SHIVA SUTRAS

What he teaches is essentially a mix of psychological, yogic and meditation exercises tinged with the latest management jargon. *India Today*

He is the latest Guru on the corporate scene. And his program on Stress and Creativity are being lapped up by executives from top-notch companies. *Business World*

TOI does a poll on who talks the talk best. Swamiji tops the list on all counts. This is one man who has the abillity to reach out to every member in the audience. Swamiji is erudite, often lyrically so. His programs have been consciously designed to suit the widest spectrum of people, to keep metaphysical and semantic speculations to the minimum. *The Times of India*

Swamiji adopts interactive mode than preaching or discourse mode so that the individual comes out to enquire into the problems or situations with openness and seek their own solutions. He uses objective perception of human problems, realities of life, relationships and situations encountered in life. *Business Line*

Swamiji is clear about what ails the corporate world and its generals; the soul-sapping constant struggle to be one up on the competitor. He is attempting what no corporate guru has ever tried; reconcile two conflicting objectives. Be a gladiator in the violence-filled arena of corporate competition and yet be at peace within. *Business Standard*

Swamiji reveals mentally and socially challenging tasks important to success such as decision making, the divine principle of worldly achievement, mind management and powerful art of goal setting. *Home News Tribune, USA*

SHIVA SUTRAS

Divine Techniques for
Enhancing Effectiveness

SWAMI
SUKHABODHANANDA

JAICO PUBLISHING HOUSE

Ahmedabad Bangalore Bhopal Chennai
Delhi Hyderabad Kolkata Mumbai

Published by Jaico Publishing House
A-2 Jash Chambers, 7-A Sir Phirozshah Mehta Road
Fort, Mumbai - 400 001
jaicopub@jaicobooks.com
www.jaicobooks.com

Published in arrangement with
Prasanna Trust
No. 51, 16th Cross, Between 6th & 8th Main
Malleswaram, Bangalore 560 055, India

SHIVA SUTRAS
ISBN 978-81-7992-979-7

First Jaico Impression: 2009
Second Jaico Impression: 2009

Printed by
Rashmi Graphics
#3, Amrutwel CHS Ltd., C.S. #50/74
Ganesh Galli, Lalbaug, Mumbai-400 012
E-mail: tiwarijp@vsnl.net

About the Author

Swami Sukhabodhananda is the founder Chairman of Prasanna Trust. He is also the founder of the research wing of Prasanna Foundation, which focuses on the scientific aspects of meditation.

His several books have made many discover a new way of living life. He makes you realise that if one door closes another door opens. Life is an opening.

He is a regular invitee to various forums in India, USA, UK, and Switzerland.

He has been addressing many gatherings at important Universities in India and abroad.

Leading industrial houses invite him to conduct 'In-house workshops' for their executives.

His self-development programs have benefited many in the corporate sectors of reputed institutions like banking, finance, industry, education, armed forces and police.

"Times of India" in their recent poll on "who talks the best" places Swamiji as the one, who tops the list on all counts as the best speaker.

"The Week" magazine acclaims Swamiji as one among the top five best exponent of spiritual knowledge.

Swamiji's English books "Oh, Mind Relax Please!" and "Oh, Life Relax Please!" are the top best sellers in the country and has set a new bench mark in the lives of many, from the Kargil hero Gen. V. P. Malik who swears by the inspiring content of the book to the New York Mayor who acknowledges its usefulness to diminish work pressure and dealing with New York City press!

His other English books are marching best sellers.

Swamiji's book "Manase Relax Please" has set an all time sales record in the history of Tamil, Kannada & Telugu books and has been included as a part of curriculum in some of the schools & colleges. Leading personalities have termed that he has revolutionized Tamil literature through his books.

Swamiji was invited as a dignitary on five different panels at the World Economic Forum in Davos, Switzerland and was a special invitee to the United Nation World Millennium Summit of spiritual Leaders.

Swamiji is the only Hindu monk who was invited to participate in the program "Eye on India" showcasing the country by CNN.

Swamiji's works in audio and video have been transforming the lives of many through Sa Re Ga Ma and Times Music.

His message on the Astha, Gemini, Sadhana, DD Chandana, World Space Radio and many other Channels is reaching a wide spectrum of people both in India and Overseas.

Swamiji was awarded 'Karnataka's Best Social Service Award' by Essel group & Zee network.

From the Author

I have always inspired myself that if I cannot be happy "here and now," I will never be happy anywhere. This book is an offering of my insights to create happiness in all walks of life. This is possible if one looks at life in a new way ... looking at life differently.

The superficial way of reading this book is through intellectual understanding. The deeper way is by feeling the insights of the narration. The deepest way is where these insights and parables light up your mind & heart in your hours of darkness and guide you like a spiritual friend.

Hence I invite you to read this book not just once, but

many times over like a daily prayer ... for prayer does not change the Lord but changes you.

By ingesting the essence of this book, you will realise what lies before you and behind you are nothing in comparison to what lies within you. Enlightenment is looking for spectacles that sit right on your nose. Enlightenment is always "here and now," never in the past or future. This book attempts to awaken you ... like a wake up call.

To do what you like and like what you do is indeed a divine work. Work is an opportunity to find oneself. This book helps you in finding your "self" in all walks of life ... family, work, social, and spiritual zones. In the process, you will be grateful to the weeds of your mind. They ultimately help your practice of relaxation.

Being relaxed is wise. Begin with being wise and you will be relaxed. Being relaxed is a wise and an easy way to live life. When you are relaxed, you look at life differently.

Life, thus lived will bring forth the peace of a rose garden and light of the luminous Sun as a part of your being.

Let your growth bring the best seasons of your life. This is my humble prayer for you.

I specially thank P. R. Madhav for editing this book. My special thanks to Mrs. Devki Jaipuria for all her support. My salutation to my loving mother who is the source of my inspiration. My deepest gratitude, which cannot be expressed in words, goes out to all my Gurus. I offer this book to all my students who are like little lamps shining in the night, which the great Sun cannot do. This is my dream and I am sure you will join me in making it as your destination.

With blessings,

SWAMI SUKHABODHANANDA

Contents

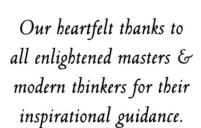

*Our heartfelt thanks to
all enlightened masters &
modern thinkers for their
inspirational guidance.*

I

Bharat – India is a Vision and Experience

I am extremely honoured and with humility, say fortunate, to unfold the rare text on Shiva sutras. I would not like to go into the history of the word 'Shiva Sutra' or where it comes from but the word Shiva means '*Sham mangalam karoti iti shiva*'.

Please understand – *sham* means *mangalam*, *karoti* means that which creates *mangalam*, or in other words that which creates auspiciousness. It is similar to the word Krishna which means '*Aakarshnam iti Krishna*' – which I have unfolded during my discourses on Bhagavad Gita. Look at Lord Krishna. His presence is *aakarshanam* – that which attracts. I would like all of you to understand that we need to invoke the state of consciousness of Lord Krishna, or Lord Shiva more than their physical form.

Lord Krishna, Lord Shiva and Lord Buddha are not just objects to be merely worshipped. Worshipping them and stopping then worshipping them is belittling the very vision and experience of all these great souls.

Lord Krishna is a state of being, Lord Shiva is a state of being, and so are Lord Buddha and Lord Mahaveera. It is a state of consciousness. And this consciousness is *avaahanam* — to be invoked.

Take, for example, Lord Krishna. If you are a true devotee of Lord Krishna, you will see the quality of Lord Krishna as *Ananda Lahari, Prema Lahari* and *Soundarya Lahari. Lahari* means waves and his presence is like waves of *Ananda* or joy; waves of *Prema* or love and waves of *Soundarya* or beauty because he represents elegance in perfection, elegance in every piece of marvelous creation.

A person living in that state creates an *oorjha* — an energy field. Such energy field of Lord Krishna is aakarshanam. So when we worship Lord Krishna, we pray for his blessings and at the same time; seek that state of consciousness which we have to reach. It is the *paramatma*... the higher self that exists in us.

Similarly, Shiva means *sham mangalam karoti* – *sham* means mangalam or auspiciousness, karoti – His presence creates auspiciousness everywhere.

Lord Shiva represents three Shaktis – Strengths... *Ichcha Shakti, Kriya Shakti* and *Vidya Shakti*. *Ichcha Shakti* means His intention is beautiful; His intention is to destroy the ratri or darkness in us.

On Shivaratri day we say, the night or darkness in us has to be destroyed. One of the Upanishads beautifully states – we are always outgoing. If we closely observe we find how effortlessly our minds are rooted outwardly.

Parānche khāni vyatrnat swaymbhih
Tasmāt paran pasyati
Na antarātman
Kaschit dhirah pratyagatmānam aikshat
Avrttacakshuh amrtatvam icchan

The Kathopanishad declares *Parānche khāni* – always outgoing. If one observes closely our mind wanders on various objects. . . without any effort at all. And this process just goes on and on. To go inside or to look inside one needs to be a *sakshi* – witness of the mind, which in other words is the witness of the thought. To go inside and look within one needs to put in a lot of effort.

Let us understand that our minds wandering outside is very natural, but to go inside is not natural, but an extraordinary excellence that one needs to bring in life. And in such extraordinary excellence, can one really enhance the quality of consciousness?

Let us take the word Bharat... Bharat means India. Bharat is more than geography. Bharat is a vision, Bharat is an experience. What is Bharat? *Brahma vidhyam tasyam ramate iti bharata.*

Brahma vidhyam — one who revels in ultimate truth, *tasyam ramate* — one who is always reveling in what the truth is... that is Bharat. So more than geography, Bharat is a vision. India is a vision.

Similarly, Lord Krishna is more than a physical presence. He is a vision. Lord Krishna says, "*Avajananthi Mam moodaha manushim tanu ashritaha*". *Avajananthi means* they really don't know me. *Manushim tanu* means they look at me as a body *Avajananthi mam moodaha* means they are indeed fools. In short, they are fools who look at me as a mere physical body.

I am unfolding a vision, of experience because the whole vision of Indian culture is to transform from *samsara* — bondage to *nirvana* — freedom.

We are in a state of *samsara*... always in deficiency. Nirvana is a state of internal sufficiency. To experience sufficiency in our lives is the overall vision.

To dwell deeply let us start with Shivaratri because all of us understand this well, as most of us celebrate Shivaratri festival. I remember as a young boy, we used to wait for Shivaratri, because special movie shows were available all through the night in the theatres. Why? Because we have to be awake throughout the night on Shivaratri. Can you see how foolishly we live? And when we are awake, we watch a movie or play cards. That is not the way to celebrate Shivaratri festival.

Ratri means there is darkness inside us. There is ignorance of our higher nature. There is a centre in us which is uncontaminated by the world. What do we do? We have to destroy the darkness. But how? How do we destroy the darkness? By bringing in *Ichcha Shakti*, *Vidya Shakti* and *Kriya Shakti* as a part of our daily lives.

Lord Krishna represents *Ananda Lahari*, *Prema Lahari* and *Soundarya Lahari* while Lord Shiva represents three shaktis — *Ichcha Shakti*, *Vidya Shakti* and *Kriya* Shakti.

Let us take up *Ichcha Shakti*. *Ichcha* means one's intention. What should be one's intention? Not just pleasure, name, fame or acquire more money. This is an ordinary

intention. But if one brings in Lord Shiva's energy – that
is *mangalam* and continues to acquire pleasure, name,
fame or more money there is nothing wrong but go a
little higher, to the next level.

What is the next level? One's *Ichcha Shakti* should be to
destroy the internal darkness. Who really am I? God
gives us a trailer of this every night. When we go to
sleep, the state of sleep is such a magical state. The state
of sleep is so magical, so aesthetical, no money can ever
buy it. It is natural and allows us to be with ourselves.
But only thing is that we are ignorant.

The great saint Patanjali said that there is difference
between *Nidra* and *Samadhi* – enlightened consciousness.
In *Nidra* you are asleep. In *Samadhi* you are in a conscious
state.

Therefore on Shivaratri festival, there is a ratri, there is
a night, there is a darkness; to that darkness one need
to bring the quality of Lord Shiva... mangalam.

Lord Shiva is not darkness. I was so surprised to hear
in one of the discourses, Shiva being called a dark night.
Shiva is not a dark night. Shiva means *mangalam*. The
speaker is misrepresenting Shivaratri with 'Shiva as dark
night.' Shiva, the word, means *mangalam* – into the dark
night of one's soul, bring the consciousness of Lord
Shiva. And what is the consciousness of Lord Shiva? It
is *mangalam*, it is auspiciousness. *Ichcha Shakti* means one's

intention to destroy the internal darkness. Keep the intention alive.

When Wright Brothers thought about a plane, they only intended to create a plane. When they had the intention to create a plane, they did not have the knowledge to create a plane. Did they have? They only had the intention. And from that intention to build a plane, they acquired necessary knowledge and experimented. Rest is history.

Therefore, the mother of creativity is a pure intention.

So the first quality of Lord Shiva which brings *mangalam* - auspiciousness is *Ichcha Shakti*. With this intention, the very effort stated in one of the sutras of Lord Shiva is, *Udhyamo Bhairavaha*. *Udhyamo* means the very effort that one creates, an intention to eliminate darkness... such effort is called *Udhyamo*; *Bhairavaha* means Lord Shiva — it means the very intention itself is Lord Shiva... *mangalam*.

There was an old Sufi lady who read that prayers move mountains. In her backyard there was a mountain covering a river. So she sat down, closed her eyes and prayed, 'Let the mountain move, let the mountain move, let the mountain move. By God's blessings, let the mountain move so that I can

see the river.' For fifty minutes she prayed and when she
opened her eyes. What did she see? The mountain was
exactly where it was. She smiled and said, "I was cocksure
that this mountain would not move." That means her
prayer came with the conviction that even prayers cannot
work.

This is how most of us pray. This is not the spirit of
prayer.

Please understand that when you are reading this book,
many of you should audit yourself, and edit yourself.
You sit down and say 'Let me collect all this information.
In the next birth I will practice them.' This would not
work.

One of the reasons why Hindus are very relaxed people
is because they believe in rebirth. Whereas Christians and
Mulisms do not believe in rebirth and they have to
complete their understanding in this very birth. They
don't know whether eternally they will be in heaven or
hell. But for Hindus it is a *pyjama* – loose philosophy.
Kindly don't operate from such philosophy.

"*Iccha Shakti*, the intention is that I am going to destroy
my ignorance right here" – such type of commitment
while sitting is called Upanishad. The word Upanishad
is the end word of Veda. The Veda has two portions

Karma Kanda and *Gnana Kanda*.

Karma Kanda is concerned with rituals while *Gnana Kanda* is concerned with knowledge which is called Upanishad. What does the word Upanishad mean? The Great saint Adi Shankaracharya says, "*Sadehe datoho* visharana gati avasadanarthsya kqup pratyaanthasya *rupam Upanishad iti*".

The Bhasya, commentary of Adi Shankaracharya states beautifully that the word Upanishad means sitting at the feet of the master. *Snad* means sitting at the feet of master, *Upa* means near, *ni* means *nischayena* – with definiteness and with tremendous commitment. *Shad* means to sit down, and with definite commitment near the master. Why near? So as to feel the master's vibration. Master is not the word, it is the vibration. More than the words, "Who you are speaks so loudly I cannot hear what you are speaking", the student may say. So the presence is more than the word.

When a student sits with deep commitment near the Master, as per great saint Adi Shankaracharya – *visarana gati avasadanam*. *Visaranam* means it will destroy. What will be destroyed? – One's ignorance; *gati* means one will reach; what will one reach? – *Moksha* or liberation.

There are three meanings for the word *shad*. *Visaranam* means destruction, *gati* means you will reach, and the third is *avasadhanam*, which means *shitali karana* — wearing out, at least your ignorance, your *samsara*, your frustration would loosen. It will wither away. It will not be cemented, it will loosen and fall away. You should stay near the teacher with definiteness.

Lord Shiva says in one of the sutras, that the very intention itself is *udhyamo bhairavaha*. The effort one is putting is *bhairavaha* — more often Lord Shiva is seen dancing. How is he dancing? *Bheejam avadhanam*. It exists as Bheeja in you, Bheeja means seed, but the seed should be *avadhanam*... it should be a meditative seed. Meditation exists in us as a seed, when we have a pure intention... *Ichcha Shakti*.

In my LIFE workshop I quote, "Can's creates success; Can't creates failure". "Come from I Can". In the management module I quote, 'Winners never Quit and Quitters never Win.' In the spiritual module please see that *Ichcha Shakti* is the right quality one need to possess.

Possessing only *Ichcha Shakti* is not enough. For example, if you have an intention to be a doctor, if you keep thinking that you will be a doctor and keep aside all the medical textbooks saying that you believe in auto suggestion, it will not work. So not only one should have *Ichcha Shakti*, but one should also have *Vidya Shakti*.

2

Clarity beyond Verbal Knowledge

Lord Shiva also represents *Vidya Shakti*. *Vidya* means understanding, *Vidya* means clarity. To have clarity, one should work on *Vidya Shakti* also.

Please understand that *Vidya* is a very profound word. Let us not get into *mimamsa* – enquiry. For the time being I will use the English word clarity. Many understand *Vidya* as knowledge.

One of the sutras of Lord Shiva in 'Shiva Sutra' declares, "*Gnanam bandhanam*". It says one's *gnanam* – knowledge is *bandhanam* – bondage. People's knowledge becomes their bondage, because knowledge is *shabdhatmakam*... it is only words and words. But the words are not the things. The description is not the described is the famous statement of Jiddu Krishnamurthy. The word water is not water. The word gulab jamoon is not gulab jamoon. Most people have knowledge as shabdas – words and only words. But the word is not the thing. The description is not the described.

And if such people are lost in knowledge – meaning in words and more words… they think they are wise. In fact they are otherwise.

It is said when Adi Shankaracharya was walking, he found an old man practicing *vyakarana* - grammar. Adi Shankaracharya said, '*Kya karna vyakarna pakad kar?*' – he did not say it in Hindi, but I am saying it in Hindi.

I wun, wul ruk, e wong, hi ouch, haya varat, lun, jabakan gadakash, jabakada dash kapajathough, *kapai shar hal…* don't think I am making some noise. These are Maheswara Sutras written by Panini.

From these Sutras, the entire edifice of Sanskrit grammar was built.

Lord Shiva playing damaru that emanates sounds like – *I wun, wul ruk, e wong, hi ouch,* – This grammar is very difficult to comprehend. As such Sanskrit grammar is very, very difficult.

Coming back to the story, this old man was practicing grammar when Adi Shankaracharya was passing by. Adi Shankaracharya said, *Bhaja Govindam Bhaja Govindam Govindam Bhaja Moodamathe* – seek the Lord, seek the Lord, don't seek the ordinary verbal knowledge. It is ok at one stage.

Let us come back to *Gnanam bandhanam*. It is very important to understand this very clearly. Most people feel that they possess knowledge because they can quote various *slokas* – verses. What a revolutionary statement *"gnanam bandhanam"* is. Sometimes Lord Shiva bhaktas say 'Oh' against Lord Krishna. Why? Because Lord Krishna says, *"Na hi jñānena sadr[am pavitramiha vidyate"* – there is nothing more *pavithra* or purer than knowledge. But Lord Shiva says, *"gnanam bandhanam"*. This dichotomy is created by the philosophers. They don't understand the intentions. I am sure you are not interested in scholarly discussions.

Let us examine what Krishna says – that *gnanam* is clarity. Not verbal knowledge. When Lord Shiva says – *"gnanam bandhanam"* meaning one's knowledge is binding, it means one has verbal knowledge, or word-meaning, for the word is not the thing. The word gulab jamoon as I told you earlier is not the gulab jamoon. So, Lord Shiva says one's knowledge is binding in such a background of understanding.

Let us pause for a while. When Lord Shiva says *Vidya Shakti*, *Vidya* is not knowledge because elsewhere Lord Shiva says knowledge is bondage. Then what is Vidya? It is clarity. When you drive you have to navigate and see where the traffic goes. Similarly, please see in life, all of you have to worship clarity and not knowledge. And for that you should be intelligent and know how to listen to words as I am talking. That is why a good speaker uses a word and before you form a conclusion, he pulls out the word. Then he uses another word and before you form a conclusion he pulls out that word too. That is when you get utterly confused.

Whenever you get confused in listening, be happy because buffalos don't get confused. Only people who think get confused. So what is the first shakti? *Ichcha Shakti*. What is the second shakti? *Vidya Shakti*. Shakti is strength, *Vidya* means clarity and not knowledge.

Please understand the words that I quote are not clarity. The word is not the *artha* – meaning. The word is only the indicator indicating the indicated, which is other than the indicator. The word is only the pointer pointing out the pointed, which is other than the pointer. Don't catch the word. Look, when I say, this is a word, don't stop at my finger now. When I say look, there is a pointer pointing out.

Sometimes my students seem to know everything. They get attached. They attend all my lectures. All the days of lecture they will sit in one particular place. When someone else occupies that place; the student says it is my place. The lecture hall is not owned by the student but they get attached.

In my books I have narrated many examples. I tell participants in my LIFE workshop, listen to me, don't catch my words, and catch my presence. Don't catch the words, catch the meaning. And the meaning cannot be caught by words. They say, 'How, Swamiji?' I will give an example to confuse them further.

There was a trader who sold rabbits. One day, he gave a rabbit to his servant and said, "Go and deliver the rabbit to a lady and bring the cash in return, without fail. Here is the address."

The servant, while going through a crowded market place, happened to collide with a man coming from the opposite direction. He fell down and the rabbit escaped from his hand.

The servant merely stood, watching the rabbit running

away. The onlookers said, "Hey, you idiot! Run and catch
the rabbit!"

But the servant said unperturbed, "So what, if the rabbit
ran away? Where will the rabbit go? I still have the
address given by my boss safe with me!"

I tell my students that what you get is the address – the
words. But the rabbit which has escaped represents Lord
Shiva.

My purpose here is not to give you knowledge about
Shiva Sutra. My purpose here is to give clarity on the
qualities of Lord Shiva. Good parenting is giving
children the clarity, because they have to navigate
through their life. You cannot give a map of 'left turn,
right turn' and ask them to drive the car. During
examination time the parents are tenser than the
children. This new trend has started recently. These days
counseling classes are conducted for parents. Why?
Children are going through the examination. But who
is going through the tension?

A student phoned up and said, "I am full of tension,
Swamiji. I have increased my dose of anti-depression, is
it OK?" I asked him why? He said, "Examination". He
is around 65 years old. "Which examination are you
attending", I asked. He replied, "6th standard". My

confusion increased. I asked further, "6th standard! but you are 65 years". He replied, "No, No, it is my grandchild's examination".

I get all my jokes observing my students. That is why I have dedicated all my books to my students. People ask me how I create examples. I tell them that my students are like an encyclopedia. They are constantly entertaining me with laughter and I am constantly getting enlightened. I thought enlightenment happened once, but it goes on happening.

Now let us dwell more on *Vidya Shakti*. I want you to be very sensitive. I never go away from the *raag* – musical note. Like a good musician singing *bhairav raag*, where he does *aalaap* but will be in *the bhairav* only. I have never gone away from the *raag* of Lord Shiva. As I am using words and I don't want you to form a conclusion, I will use another word to snatch away that word. But ultimately I want you to get the essence, the experience, the vision, the profoundity, the depth, the ecstasy, and the magnificence of the presence of Lord Shiva. Lord Shiva the one not only to be worshipped but to be invoked.

Shiva means *Ichcha Shakti* and *Vidya Shakti*. *Vidya* is clarity. In this sutra I am going to unfold and you should get the clarity. And don't be unhappy. When you go, you may not remember anything but I will be happy. Because

when you remember, you will repeat the words like a
parrot. When you don't remember, something has gone
into you wordlessly. That is why I have written a book
called Wordless Wisdom.

When you go out and your wife or girl friend asks you
what Swamiji spoke you may say, "Swamiji was... I
remember nothing". You may not remember the words,
because I would have used one word and snatched
another word. So don't get confused when you don't
remember. But something else happens inside silently.
The word will do something good like a pole vault. You
jump, and when you go to the other side you drop the
pole vault. That is how it happens. In academic study
you are interested in words, but in spiritual study you
have to drop words. That is why some of you are very
confused. In academic study you will get words. In
spiritual study you will not remember words.

Dakshinamurthy sthotra proclaims, *"Mouna vyākhyā
prakatita parabrahma tatvam yuvānam"*. Through silence, the
Guru taught the students. This means he taught
wordlessly as he used the words and snatched away the
words.

After the lecture, when you go out you may not
remember. Some seeds – *Bheejam avadhanam. Bheejam* -
some seeds would have been sown in you. How the

ankura is going to come, we do not know. How the tree is going to come, we do not know. But the tree is in the seed. You take the seed; where is the tree? The potential of tree is within you. It is for you to release the tree within you. The guru can only give seeds.

3

Wonderment – The Foundation of Life

Going further, the Lord Shiva represents *Ichcha Shakti, Vidya Shakti Kriya Shakti*. We have seen the meaning of *Ichcha Shakti* and *Vidya Shakti*. Now let us dwell on *Kriya Shakti*. After getting clarity one should act on the clarity... that is *Kriya Shakti*.

You know something and not to act on what you know, is equal to as good as not knowing. A lot of people know but they don't act on what they know. When you don't act on what you know, it amounts to you not knowing.

We all know smoking is very bad for health. In fact when you ask someone whom you know who is smoking, he

would probably give more details about the side effects
of smoking but continues to smoke.

In other words it means he has *shabdagnanam* – word
knowledge and not *arthagnanam* – true meaning. He has
only *stulagnanam* – gross understanding, not
sukshmagnanam – subtle knowledge. Knowledge does not
nècessarily become wisdom. Only *stulagnanam* is not
sufficient. From *stula* one has to transform to *sukhshma*
and then to *sukshmatara* – subtlest.

Lot of people say that they know but they don't act and
they are hypnotised by the fact that they know and the
fact is that they don't know, because their knowledge
is masquerading as ignorance. Knowledge is masquerading as ignorance pretending to be knowledge and that
is one of the greatest traps a person can get caught in.
Knowledge masquerades as ignorance and poses as
knowledge.

Lord Shiva emphasizes *Kriya Shakti* – act on what you
know as clarity. For example, let us take *Ichcha Shakti* – I
want to be enlightened – right now you act, don't
postpone, and act on it right now. *Vidya Shakti* – I am
going to get this clarity, it is with that positivity, your
life should start and you find *vismayaha yoga bhoomika*
happening right here and now.

If you are in the right track, *Vismayaha* ... means great wonderment that happens within you and that becomes your *yoga bhoomika*... the foundation on which your spiritual life is going to be built. What does this mean? Your foundation would be a great wonderment. And such wonderment is a great magic because transformation is the side effect, not the main effect. You have to only put yourself on the right track. When will the transformation occur, one does not know.

 There is a beautiful Zen story. A Zen Sanyasin – lady monk was walking alone. It was winter and was snowing. The woman wanted shelter for overnight stay. She knocked on the door of an unknown person. The master of the house opened the door and saw this woman and closed the door. This went on in several households. Nobody allowed her in because she was a woman and that too in the night; if it were a Zen monk they would have allowed him, but not a woman.

Unable to find an accommodation, finally she settled down under a tree, watching snowflakes dancing and falling. Being a Zen woman she knew the art of being empty, being inwardly void, being in the *Chidambaram* state, the *Chidakashaha* state. The snowflakes were dancing with tremendous ecstasy, with unbelievable elegance. Between the snowflakes the Zen woman saw the beautiful full moon. Thus she experienced the Zen experience — true *vismaya* — wonderment.

Out of this experience she wrote a beautiful Japanese poem, and in the poem the first thing she did was to thank each one who closed the door when she approached for overnight stay. She thanked each one of them saying, "Because of your compassionate act you have introduced me to the magical existence of nature. Because you closed the door, I was available to the poetry, the dance and exuberance of magical creations. What a great feeling!".

If one can really be open, different miracles starts happening and this is through true understanding of *Kriya Shakti*. One should act, right now. Thus, *Ichcha Shakti, Vidya Shakti and Kriya Shakti,* is indeed invoking Lord Shiva.

When these qualities in oneself surfaces out, such energy fields, *sham* means *mangalam*, *karoti* means that which creates *mangalam*, results in oorjha of Lord Shiva. Shiva is not a dark night. These qualities destroy *ratri* - ignorance inside us. Hence it is celebrated as Shivaratri.

Once in a year you make a resolution, but if you are a real *sadhaka* — seeker, every moment you should make a decision. When you start living your life on these principles, you are a true devotee of Lord Shiva. It is not just by breaking coconuts, lighting oil lamps, or by smearing *vibhuti* – holy ash. There is nothing wrong in applying *vibhuti*, but please do not stop there. With these qualities being part of life, one's life truly would transform.

 A person came to me and said, "Swamiji, you speak all these as you are a Sadhu; you don't have a wife, no children; Well, I have more than one wife, so many children, so many things. I am a very generous man; I have sown *bheeja* everywhere. You say *bheeja avadhanam*, my *bheeja* is different. All this I have done, now I face so many problems. I have to manage all of them. My religion allows more than one marriage. How many problems are there with the first wife you know? You are able to talk because you have no wife. I have to balance my first wife, second wife, third wife and hidden wife. I have not one boss, but so many bosses. What does Lord Shiva have to say on this, Swamiji?"

See what questions people ask me. You think I am telling you a joke?

I paused for a while and told him, "Look at Lord Shiva's family; though a small family, it is full of problems. What is Shiva's *vahana* – vehicle? It is Nandi – bull. Shiva's wife is Durga or Kali. What is her *vahana*? Tiger.

So the wife's *vahana* is a tiger, the husband's *vahana* is
bull. The tiger is waiting to pounce on Nandi – bull.
How many interdepartmental problems Lord Shiva must
be facing? Because of Durga the tiger is keeping quiet.
Going further, Lord Shiva's son is Ganesha. What is
Ganesha's *vahana*? Rat. What is around Shiva's neck?
Snake. The snake is waiting to eat the elder son's *vahana*.
See the magnitude of the problem. Because of Ganesha,
the rat is keeping quiet and because of Lord Shiva the
snake is keeping quiet.They all have a problem of one
consuming the other.

At least your wives are only fighting with you or amongst
themselves.

The other son of Lord Shiva is Shanmukha. His *vahana*
is the peacock and the peacock is waiting to snatch the
snake. The peacock is waiting to snatch the snake, the
snake is waiting to catch the rat, the tiger is waiting to
catch Nandi. Think of the multiple interdepartmental
problems in Lord Shiva's family. And in spite of several
problems, Lord Shiva is calm. On Lord Shiva's head
there is *Chandra* – Moon. *Chandra* represents a calm mind.
We find Ganga is flowing out of Lord Shiva's head.
What does Ganga represent? It represents river of
knowledge. The river of clarity is flowing".

It is emphasized that how to keep one's mind calm in spite of several problems.

Most of us may not have many wives but we need to understand that one wife is a multi personality or one husband can be a dominating personality. That is not the problem. Stop this illusion and delusion that when problems are not there, only then you would be happy.

Shiva Sutra can be practiced in spite of several problems. The Bhagavad Gita can be practiced in spite of many problems. You have to learn to swim in the ocean in spite of the waves. You have to swim in the river in spite of the current. You cannot say, "Let the water stop flowing then I will swim or let the water disappear, then I will swim".

How ridiculously we live our lives. I will narrate it through a story.

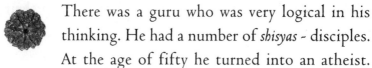 There was a guru who was very logical in his thinking. He had a number of *shisyas* - disciples. At the age of fifty he turned into an atheist. When the guru himself turned into an atheist, all the disciples thought that there was something wrong with the guru and they all left him and went away except one disciple. This was very rare for someone to stay back. That is why most of the gurus are very intelligent. They

expect you to touch the feet of the guru as a part of reverance. Just imagine what would happen if a guru's face is touched by everyone. Instead they intelligently make others touch only their feet.

In this story, only one disciple who stayed on asked the guru, "You are about to die Guruji, at least become a theist now." To which the guru replied, "God does not exist". But the disciple pleaded again. The guru said, "I think God will not pardon me, because I have turned into an atheist." The disciple replied, "God will pardon you." The disciple had now taken the role of guru.

Soon the guru died. All his earlier disciples came back to attend his funeral. They noticed fumes emanating under the carpet where his body was kept before taking out for cremation. When the fumes began to rise, the disciples realised that the guru was burning inside as God would not pardon him. The disciples prayed for the soul of the guru that God would pardon him but the soul answered back that God would not heed to their prayer. They were in a fix.

Now it was the turn of the only disciple who did not desert the guru to act on. He said, "If God does not pardon, I would pardon". The soul of the guru asked this disciple as to how he can take the role of God and pardon him. The disciple replied, "The student is pure in believing that the guru is not an atheist, when the guru is definitely a theist but pretending to be an atheist. If the student could be so pure, the guru who taught such a student must be much more. And therefore I am saying that I can forgive you".

When the story was narrated to me, something really touched. A true guru is not really interested in the crowd. There is an interesting point I would like to mention. There is what is called the body of religion, mind of religion and soul of religion. If you see the majority, they are only interested in the body of religion. Go and shave your head, smear vibhuti, break a coconut... these are all the practices which forms the body of the religion. The mind of the religion sees them in terms of - breaking the coconut means one has to break one's ego. Very few people are interested in the mind of the religion. The majority will go for physical form of worship. Few are interested in a discourse like this.

The soul of religion is – dropping the ego, dropping the mind, dropping the thought, which still few people are interested in. The real guru is one who is really interested in the people who in turn are interested in being enlightened. He is not interested in the crowd of disciples. So in the above story the guru played a strategy of becoming an atheist. And most of the disciples who said, "Oh, our Guruji has turned into an atheist" and walked away. But the only disciple knew that the guru was playing a role. Therefore that disciple said, "If I can be pure in following you, you are my guru and so how much purer you must be."

And therefore I am saying this, that God is playing a drama with all our problems.

Why is God playing a joke on you? Why is He playing a drama? In a drama you have to become better and not bitter. You have to become better and better and not bitter and bitter. And when you become better and better and not bitter and bitter, you find that a different energy will open up within you. So please drop this myth that Lord Shiva says the problem should stop, then you practice spirituality. In spite of problems you should be able to practice spirituality.

Why this problem? Don't bother why the problem. Why does moustache grow? Why is it there? How elegant it should be? I cannot answer why.

"Why have you become bald? Is it that you have less hair to comb?" But you may say, "It is because there is more face to wash." So enjoy the washing. That is why your effectiveness should have enhanced by now.

Thousands of people come and ask me why God is

playing jokes on them. Many people have told me, "Swamiji, your discourses are very good, I have heard many of them but my ignorance has not gone."

Somebody asked Buddha very beautifully, "So many people listen to you and nobody is enlightened, why?" Buddha replied, "Go and ask the devotees who have listened to my discourse, what they want?" This person went and asked all those who were attending Buddha's lecture, "What is it that you want?" One said, "I want my daughterin-law's problem to be solved", while another said, "I want more money" Everybody was telling what they want; the list included everything other than enlightenment.

He did not reveal to them that Buddha had personally asked him to find out what they want. He posed himself as a journalist. Hearing his findings Buddha answered, "They are coming to my lectures and what is their hidden agenda? Not enlightenment. Who are to be enlightened? Only those people who are interested in getting enlightened".

People came for time-pass, for spiritual entertainment.

Are you all listening? I am saying something important. So, therefore, all these problems exist. In the previous example, the guru was avoiding those disciples to identify a real disciple and in turn he found one. In spite of the master being erratic, the disciple could see the purity of the master.

In and through the waves of life, if we know the art of the elegance to swim through the waves, then we are worthy of receiving what Lord Shiva is unfolding through magical sutras.

So therefore, let us re-look at *Ichcha Shakti, Vidya Shakti, Kriya Shakti*. Look at Lord Shiva. He is holding a trident — a *trishula*. When you worship, you have to worship the qualities associated with trident. It is similar to Lord Krishna having a flute which is empty. You and I should be empty as a flute. Only then the music would flow. You and I should be empty of ego, vanity, pride. Only then God's music would flow, that is symbolic of Lord Krishna.

4

Language of Mysticism – A Calm Mind

L ord Shiva has a *trishula* – trident in His hands
which represents *the* three gunas – *Satwa guna, Rajo
guna and Tamo guna* meaning that all the three
gunas are in His hands. He is the master of the gunas
and the gunas are not the master of Him.

It is a very big topic that we would be dealing as we go
further. *Sattva* is the one pure quality, *Rajo* is the quality
of activity where ego plays a role, *Tamo* is darkness,
laziness. All three qualities have roles to play but you
should not be a victim to any one of them. Whenever
you go to sleep, it is reflection of *tamo guna*; sleep must
be part of your routine, but not right now while you are

listening to me... therefore you should have control over tamo guna.

A person said, "Swamiji, whenever I listen to you I am sleeping." The *tamo guna* was misplaced there. *Rajo guna* is sign of activity, so actively you have to sit for meditation. There is no activity in meditation, so someone goes on scratching his head, there is nothing inside and outside, but he scratches. Again *rajo guna* has been misplaced here. All these three gunas have roles to play, if you only know how to become the master and not the victim. For that to happen those roles have to be played in the respective places. For some people *Sattva guna* — purity becomes addiction.

I will narrate an example from the life of Buddha so that you can understand better.

Four people were in a boat. On reaching the shore, they were holding the boat on their heads and started walking. A monk who saw this asked, "Why are you keeping the boat on your heads"? They said, "The boat has helped us to cross the river and we are so grateful to the boat that we are carrying the boat wherever we go".

After the boat is used, it should be anchored on the

shore. These people out of gratitude carried the boat on their heads.

Have you seen some people expressing their gratitude? For them their gratitude itself is a form of bondage. Similarly, the very gratitude became bondage for those four people.

If you have *yagnopavitha* – sacred thread on you, and when you take *sanyas* – monk hood, as per the tradition, you have to tear them down. It is verydifficult as you have been wearing the *yagonopavitha* all through your life and chanting the Gayatri Mantra. It is treated as very sacred throughout the life and when you take *sanyasa* the *yagnopavitha* has to be torn by our own hands... even that attachment has to be renounced. Even the attachment to good, along the line, should go away.

Buddha said that gratitude is beautiful, but don't be foolish like the boatmen carrying the boat in the name of gratitude. Then the boat becomes a burden instead of a means of navigation.

Therefore one should be a master of all the three *gunas* – qualities. You should be able to leave off, that is the meaning of *trishula* or trident.

What is there on the *trishula?* A *Damaru* – a drum tied

to it. The whole system of Sanskrit grammar seems to have emerged from the *damaru*, discovered by the great Saint called Panini. It is said that he wanted to write grammar sutras. He was meditating calmly for this purpose. At that time the intuitive quadrant of his brain opened up very well. He seemed to have tuned to the celestial dance of Lord Shiva during the *sandhya* – evening time. It is said that Lord Shiva was dancing with his *damaru* and thus Panini sutras were created.

I want you to know a little of Indian culture. Just 'Be Indian, buy Indian' is not enough. 'I ate masala dosa, Swamiji, therefore I am Indian. I ate pani-puri, therefore I am a Sindhi.'

Panini was a great saint. He was meditating. Why am I naratting this? The fine vibration is there in this world. Akashvani waves are right here, BBC waves, CNN waves, Doordarshan waves are here, but your radio or TV with antenna alone can pick it up. I am giving you a modern example. They will help you to understand an ancient concept, because you are all westernised.

How did Panini get the idea when Lord Shiva was dancing? How is it that you type www. swamisukhabodhananda.org and you get my site? You say, "Oh, It is like that. Isn't it?" Right here we have BBC, CNN, and Doordarshan waves and if you have the right receiver, you can log on to it, isn't it?

A study has shown that whatever the great Kishore Kumar has sung, or for that matter whatever great singers have sung, it can never disappear; it is always in existence. And we create an apparatus, and we can log on to it. Energy cannot be destroyed. It exists in some form or the other. We don't have the apparatus right now to discover them. That is all. Therefore, meditation is an apparatus and in the apparatus are your receptors of intuition, which modern science refers as the "D" quadrant of your brain.

There are four quadrants of brain – "A" quadrant is of logic, "B" quadrant is of planning, "C" quadrant is of kinesthetic and playful while "D" quadrant is of intuition. "D" quadrant of the brain represents intuition.

When you meditate, research has shown that the intuition brain cells opens up, and then you see more than what others can see. That is why Walt Disney looked at the rat and created Mickey Mouse. Somebody looks at waste and creates wealth.

When great Saint Panini was meditating, his receptors opened so well and it is said he was tuned to Lord Shiva's dance with *damaru*. Panini captured the sound right there and immediately wrote it down. This is called Maheswara

Sutra on which the entire edifice of Sanskrit grammar
is built. And the majestic, most marvellous system of
literature on grammar created. Therefore see the sounds
now. I repeat it. See the sound of the *damaru*.

I wun, wul ruk, e wong, hi ouch, haya varat, lun,jabakan
gadakash, jabakada dash kapajathough, *kapai shar hal*... iti
Maheswara sutrani.

After you learn this by heart, it takes about twelve years
to understand the meaning. What can you and I learn?
Panini could learn. But what can we learn from this?

The other saint, Patanjali, through his intuition, decoded
Panini's sutras. Saint Patanjali who wrote the Yoga
sutras, through his intuition, wrote the meaning of the
Maheswara sutras, which is called the Patanjali
commentaries.

Whether in Vaishnva system or Shaivite system or
anyother, *Mahabhashyakara* means Saint Pathanjali only.
When we say *Bhashyakara*, it means either Shankaracharya
or Ramanujacharya depending on the school of
philosophy. But 'Great commentaries' means it is
Patanjali's commentaries on the Panini sutras only.
Without this, we could not have understood Sanskrit
grammar at all. I have studied both systems of

philosophy. The logical sequence of them, is mind-boggling.

What you have to understand is that mystical sounds exist in this world of creation. If you can be like Panini... be very calm, serene, tranquil, then there is a possibility that you can log on to the mystical sound. Like in the earlier example the Zen woman who was grateful to those who refused to provide accommodation, because of which she was able to see something bigger.

You can also be calm and serene, with commitment. *Bheejam Avadhanam.* This is very important sutra from Shiva Sutra. *Bheejam* means seed, *avadhanam* means *dhyanam*. So meditation is a seed; it means your life should be one of meditation and the meditation should be the seed. If you want to grow a tree in your garden you have to first sow the seed. Similarly, meditation should be the seed.

What is meditation? For the time being, understand that meditation is heightened awareness where your mind is very, very calm. *Bheejam Avadhanam. Bheejam,* your seed should be meditation. One of the reason I chose the title of my first book as Manase, Relax Please and in Hindi, it is called Man Re, Relax Please and in English, Oh, Mind Relax Please!

Wherever you are, whoever you are, whatever is your profession, you may be anybody, remember meditative energy should be your seed. Whatever you are meditating on should be your root. Therefore, when Panini was very calm, he was able to capture Lord Shiva's *damaru* sound. Patanjali was very calm, and so he could interpret Panini's sutras, which we are able to read. The only system of grammar available right now is the Panini system. In fact, there were nine systems of grammar and we have lost eight of them. We have references that say Hanuman had mastered nine systems of grammar. Fortunately we have at least one system left.

You and I can be calm, serene and tranquil, for that should be our commitment…that should be our *bheeja*. Every moment *bheeja* should be very calm, *bheejam avadhanam*. You may have a lot of problems, but you can still be calm and if you are calm, you will learn something.

How did Panini get these sutras? When you are calm, you can log on. Unless you are calm, it will look like gibberish and you will understand nothing. But Patanjali was so evolved that he could decode the sutras. So the decoding language of mysticism is the calm mind.

Saint Kabir says, *"Is Gat Ander anahath gar jai isme utatu puhar"*.

"Is gat ander" means *"is shareer ke bheethar, anahath garjai"*.
Anahath means silence, *garjai* is roaring, *isme utatu puhar* –
like the fountain, the silence is roaring, but one's mind
should be calm. But unfortunately, Kabir says, our mind
is not calm.

"Chalti chakki dekhake dhiya kabira roi, do patan *ke beech
me sabut bacha na koi."*

If you are a true Shiva bhakta, you can be rooted to
bheejam avadhanam. The mind needs to be calm. When the
damaru sounds are heard in a calm mind, they are
mystical sounds.

Whenever I give discourse, I prepare for my talk, but
what I have prepared and what I talk are entirely
different. My mother keeps asking, "Why are you
preparing?" I say, "I do not know why I prepare?" Because
when one is calm, suddenly from somewhere, you catch
an understanding.

That is why they say before you sit down on the seat of
unfoldment, touch the seat with reverence or bow down
to the seat with reverence as it is called as "Vyasa peeta".
As per the tradition it is said every person who gives
good discourses is blessed by the saints.

If you ask good speakers they will say they do not know

where the ideas came from, where the thought came from. It comes because of the energy field, the vibration, the mystical sounds that exists. My students who take Mantra Yoga also tell me, "Swamiji, suddenly it appears as though you are speaking through us."

Please understand that it is not who is speaking through my students. When the mind is calm, you are able to log on to those frequencies. When your mind is restless you are not able to do so.

What can one learn from the *damaru* of Lord Shiva? Keep your mind calm and mystical sounds happen within you. Don't start thinking that by keeping calm, nothing is heard, only a buzzing sound is coming up, so new tension starts.

A person shared that his only tension was getting enlightenment and he had no other tension. Search for enlightenment should reduce the tension. Another person came and told me that every day he feels like taking bath twenty times. I was confused. Heasked me whether it is practical to take bath twenty times a day. I asked him how many times he actually took bath. To ask this question, I had to push my way through his words. He said not even once he had taken bath twenty times. He was worried about why he got the thought of taking bath twenty times. I told him, "Taking bath is not a problem, you are the problem." He was only making that an issue.

Please get this right now and keep the mind calm. One says his only tension is enlightenment. If so drop it. Don't make it an issue. There are some people. To have no problems is a problem for them. Their biggest problem is that they have no problem. So they go on generating problems like Ravana's head. See, enlightenment is the new problem. Now, don't convert this to a problem. When your mind is calm, it will capture the mystical sounds. Don't say, "But when, Swamiji? Come and tell us quickly." Drop this expectation.

Just be calm. And when you are calm, even if you get a heart attack, you will say, "Hey, I got a heart attack, I wonder why?" Someone was telling me, "Oh, my life style was different." Somebody else recently told a person who had had a heart attack that it was not because his life style was different but because his working style is different. Everything creates tension. How to be calm is also a source of tension for some. You may think that I am cracking a joke. But I have told you that my students are my greatest source of enlightenment. Through my students I get more enlightenment than from the Shiva Sutras. Seeing their problems, I find that I have no problems at all. A grey haired man once asked me, "Is there a mantra to get rid of the grey hair, any sutra, Swamiji, for the grey hair to disappear?" He does not see that my hair has turned grey handling him.

5

A Divine Technique to Transform You

Going further, what is Lord Shiva seated on? A Tiger skin. The tiger is a very symbolic. The tiger represents aggression, because we have to attack our ignorance. The tiger stands for vision. When a tiger wants to attack, it positions itself carefully and focuses on the object it wants. Even if some other animal comes near it, it will not be distracted, it will just go towards the object it focuses on and invariably gets it. The tiger is not distracted by other objects... whereas some people get disturbed by the slightest distraction.

One day, a man told me that every woman he met, he felt like the most beautiful woman he had met. I asked

him why he felt like that. "What can I say, Swamiji?
Every woman is more beautiful than the other woman."
I told him that he would never get married if he is like
this.

The tiger is so focused on the particular object it wants
and is sure of getting it. So, what you should learn from
the tiger is to have a focused vision. You and I should
focus on our *moola avidya*. There are two types of *avidya*.
Moola avidya means root ignorance. What is our basic
ignorance?

What is *moola avidya*? Everybody has *moola avidya*. For
some people, there appears many thoughts, which when
they decode, will reduce to one or two basic thoughts.
It appears like many thoughts. The tiger focuses on the
herd of deer and comes to one deer as its focus for the
kill. Many thoughts may be there in you, but if you
decode you will come to one or two thoughts. But for
some people it can only be sex. Sex can only be one
thought. And from the *moola avidya* of sex thought they
will have a variety of various thoughts. How can you
handle many thoughts? I tell them to forget about many
thoughts, instead to dig and find out which is the basic
thought. For some people it is sex, for some people it
is anger, for some people it is jealousy, for some people
it is power game, for some it is only name and fame.
That is the *moola avidya* — the basic thought from which

branches come out. If you get lost in the branches, you will miss the root.

Do you understand what I am saying? And if you don't understand, don't worry, relax. If it is not possible in this birth, there are many more births. I really mean it.

Lord Shiva is seated on a tiger skin. What is the quality of the tiger? If there is a herd of deer, it focuses on one and attacks it, even when other deer is near it. How do we apply this in our lives? We have so many thoughts. Many thoughts are like many deer. Focus on what? One. What is your root *avidya, moola avidya*? In Vedanta, *moola avidya* is very important discipline to recognize in oneself.

The Bhagavad Gita states, *"Agnyanena tu gnanam avrutam tena muhyanthi jantavaha..."* Your ignorance covers your intellect because of which you are deluded.

So the first thing that we must remember is tiger stands for focus.

Second, the tiger stands for power. It has tremendous power. And Lord Shiva is seated on a tiger skin. You and I should have the power of commitment. See, even marriage also works on commitment. One man asked, "Why should I have commitment? My commitment is not to have commitment. What do you say?" I said perfectly fine. I would not like to play logic with words now.

Nothing is achieved without commitment. Even spirituality is achieved through commitment. Marriage works on commitment. Any scientific discovery requires commitment. Therefore, the tiger represents power. You and I should have the power of commitment. You may put so much of effort, but what is required is total commitment.

There once lived a famous grammarian called Dixit. He did not believe in God. He was very well known for his knowledge. But his father was very unhappy with him because his father was a great believer in God but it was not so with the son. Everyday, the father would visit the temple. The father was disappointed with the son for not visiting the temple, not believing in God. The son told the father that he had heard him saying Rama, Rama, Rama many a times but there was no change at all in him. Seeing the father, the son's belief in God had also disappeared. In spite of going to the temple, the father was still poor, while the temple was getting richer.

Years passed. The father was on his deathbed. He said to his son, "My last wish is to see you visit the temple and utter Lord Rama's name."

Dixit was a noble man and he replied, "Ok, I will visit the temple, but I will not utter Lord Rama, Rama, Rama like you; instead I will say Rama once in *bahuvachan* — meaning in plural. In Sanskrit *Ramaha, Ramov...* means many Ramas. So why should I say Rama, Rama, Rama? I will say in *bahuvachan* once and God will multiply it because grammatically it is correct." After all, Dixit was a grammarian. The father said that *bahuvachanam* or *ekavachanam* did not matter. Dixit went to the temple but never returned. He said *Ramaha* so profoundly that he became *aikya* — one with the Lord Rama and seemed to have breathed his last.

People who saw this narrated the incident to the father. The son, Dixit was no more. Dixit said *Ramaha* only once and he just got lost in the Lord. The father said, "My son must have said it with so much *prana* — life, that he was so totally involved in it. That his utterance *Ramaha* once was enough whereas I have been superficially saying Rama, Rama, Rama, and so my *samsara* still exists. My son said it only once, and he lost in it."

If only we can get that totality. In the story when we say Dixit died, it means he became *aikya* — one with the Lord. It only means living in total. Your commitment should be so total, that the power of commitment should lead you to enlightenment with that totality.

One should have the vision first, the power next and the commitment thereafter.

What else does the tiger have? Speed. So the next quality
is speed. The tiger possess tremendous speed. We should
also practice spirituality with speed. All of us have
already one foot placed in the grave. Every lorry in the
city of Mumbai looks like a *Yama dootha* – messenger of
Lord Death. The shape of Indian lorries is very
appropriately created. It is not like in the West. There
the trucks are so colorful that you like and fall in love
with them. Here the lorries look like representative of
death. They have a very rustic look and death can strike
any moment. So where can we practice spirituality?
Right here, with speed. At once, people may say, "No,
Swamiji, my horoscope clearly says that I will live for
eight five and half years; first the astrologer who
predicted this will die and then I will die."

Have you seen some astrologers talk on TV, as if they
are Gods? And fools follow whatever they say. They tell
someone to break the left door and by doing so the
neighbour would die. The person follows the prediction
in total. Instead of the neighbour dying, he finds the
neighbour is actually getting married.

People's gullibility has no limits. Please understand that
we are in the presence of death, any moment we are going
to die. Do not say that you are going to live eighty five
and half years. Even if you are going to live eighty five
and half years, break this way of thinking and think

about how to practice spirituality right now.

I will teach you a simple technique. What does 85 years consist of? One year has 365 days, one year means 12 months, one month has 30-31 days, and one day is 24 hours. So for every year of the 85 years, start your practice with one hour; for every hour start with one minute; for every minute, start with one moment – and that moment is now. Therefore the speed should be right now. You have to practice spirituality with speed.

So, the qualities that we need to imbibe are – first is vision, second is power, third is commitment, fourth is speed, and fifth is strategy. Observe closely. When a tiger attacks, it applies strategy. If you study animals properly you will understand their strategies. In our lives too, you and I should adopt strategy to destroy our enemies. Our greatest enemy is our ignorance. We should have a strategy. The teachings of Shiva Sutra, the teachings of Brahma Sutras, are all about strategy. Right now I am teaching and all of you think you are listening. There is a silent strategy that I am supposed to expose you to; there is a tradition of teaching. I know many gurus teach because they have *shishyas* - disciple but I am exposed to a tradition of teaching, and not just talking.

There is a tradition of teaching called *adhyaropa apavada nyaya and indu shaka nyaya*. There is a strategy in teaching.

The classical style of studying scriptures is fortunately available... they are *adhyaropa apavada nyaya and indu shaka nyaya*. We apply the strategies of different *nyayas*. To handle your ignorance, you need to have a strategy.

And if you are exposed to a guru, you will understand the strategy. Therefore, the Upanishad says, *"Acharyavaan purushaha veda"*. If you have a guru you will definitely know which guru knows classical literature. Not any guru, but *acharyavaan purushaha veda* for the classical literature style of unfoldment.

As I said earlier, you should develop a strategy to handle your ignorance. The first is vision, second is power, third is commitment, fourth is speed, fifth is strategy, and sixth is skill.

If you observe closely, you find the tiger possess tremendous skill. You can consider any animal; here as Lord Shiva sits on a tiger skin, we have taken the tiger as an example. It is skilled and we see it in the way it runs, the way it positions itself, the way it attacks and turns in mid air. Every animal has skill. That is why all postures in yoga are of animal postures - *bhujangasasna, sarpasana, makarasana or mayurasana*. Our *rishis* — saints knew that one can learn so much from animals. There is a skill in each animal, you have to practice spirituality in learning a skill.

There are a lot of people who practice spirituality. One person came to me recently. His eyes were like a dragon's or dracula's eyes. He said, "Swamiji, recently, I got the experience of enlightenment. Do you see it in me, Swamiji?" He wanted confirmation from me. I said that I was enlightened to see his enlightenment. He said he practiced spirituality. Do you know what he did? From the Bhagavad Gita he took the quote *nasikagram;* the literal meaning is to concentrate on the tip of the nose and this man had for many hours focused his eyes on the tip of the nose. Grammatically he was correct, but by doing this, his eyes had been affected. One of my students asked, "What is this, Swamiji?" I told him that his English may be very good but he should read the scriptures under proper guidance.

You cannot read a book and perform surgery. Even though technically concentrating on the tip of the nose is mentioned in the Gita, what Lord Krishna said was that truth is right in front of you, just as your nose is in front of you. Whatever twisting you do, your nose will always be in front of you and never go behind. Similarly, God is always in front of you, *nasikagram.*

If you act with conviction that God is in front of you and when really God comes face to face with you, *wah,* with what *adbhuta,* with what *vinaya,* with what *bhakti,* with what *shraddha,* with what *astha,* you are going to *avahanam,* welcome every moment of life! Feel the moment of God in that moment... *avahanam samarpayami*. That is how we invoke the Lord.

Just imagine God comes face to face with you. I am sure this audience has tremendous reverence. If you treat that moment with innocence, bhakti, shraddha, my God, if you treat every moment as if this moment is God, then God will dance right in front of you.

I am giving you clarity and not criticising anybody. I saw recently on a TV show, a guru glorifying the fact that he does not know the scriptures. He talked without knowing while I am talking with my experience. You can learn to focus and learn the skill of living – the skill of living spiritually from moment to moment. You have to begin this moment because you may live for eighty years, but eighty years have to be reduced to one year, one year has to be reduced to one day, one day has to be reduced to one hour, and one hour has to be reduced to one second. So therefore, in that second you have to live. How to live the second, not with tension, but in a relaxed manner is what you should learn.

Are you getting this knack? Lord Shiva is seated on the tiger skin. What are the six things to be learnt from looking at a tiger? Values like vision, power, commitment, speed, strategy and skill. Your spiritual practices should be based on these six principles. And in such a state, *bheejam avadhanam*. This understanding should be your *bheeja* and what you should do with this bheeja is, *avadhanam*, it should become a *dhyanam* – meditation. Let all these become *bheeja* and you should meditate on this *bheeja*, you should become pregnant with these *bheeja*, you should be pregnant with the Lord and then the child would be born. *Janmana sarvey shudraha karmana brahmana bhavanti*.

By birth, everybody is a *shudra*, one belongs to lower strata of the society and by karma – good actions one changes; that is why a Brahmin, one belong to higher strata of the society is called *dwija* for *dwija* is twice born. Once you see Lord Shiva like this, then you take the *bindu* and you put it as your third eye. This eye is an eye of intuition, this becomes your *bheeja* and it should be *avadhanam*. Once you become *bheeja avadhanam*, meditation should become your seed.

6

Guru – The Inner Compass

Whenever you look at Lord Shiva, look at him deeply with meditation. Look at the *trishula* – trident meditatively, and when you offer flowers to Lord Shiva, do so meditatively. And when you offer a flower, even the offering of the flower should be done meditatively. A beautiful poem would arise in your heart:

Ahimsa prathamam pushpam, pushpam indriya nigraham, sarvabhoota daya pushpam, kshama pushpam visheshataha, shanti pushpam tapo pushpam, dhyanam pushpam tataiyacha, satyam astavidam pushpam, vishnuho preeti karambhavet.

When we offer a flower, we invoke eight important

gunas. *Ahimsa pratamam pushpam* is the first and we will dwell on this a little later. That should be the *bheeja*, when you offer a flower – *Bheejam avadhanam* – and we will see how even this can be a meditative act.

Ahimsa prathamam pushpam – what pleases Lord Shiva or Lord Vishnu is ahimsa. It is not just the flower, but the very quality of the person who offers the flower.

So, *bheejam avadhanam* – meditation should become one's way of life.

The sutras are maxims filled with a lot of meaning. They are not elaborated but are highly condensed. So sutras are to be shaken well to extract their meaning and to understand them in totality.

What I was unfolding earlier was about the sutra even though I did not quote from the sutra; I was only unfolding it. Now I am going to mention about the sutra. This style of teaching is called *Adhyaropa apavada nyaya* and *Indu shaka nyaya*. These are the two important styles of teaching in classical literature.

Indu shaka nyaya means you want to know the Indu the moon, you want to see the moon. Imagine you have never seen the moon and you ask your guru about it. The guru is going to say, "See the vriksha, see the tree, see the branches." Now you may get worked up and say, "I want to see the moon, why are you telling me to see the tree and the branches?" But that is the classical style of teaching. If you want to see the moon and you don't know what the moon is, you don't even know which direction to look in, the guru tells you to see the tree, because you know the tree – the vriksha. So the Guru starts off with what the student knows. If the Guru starts off with what he knows, then the student does not know anything. If he is going to talk on something that he knows and the student does not know, there is no communication between the guru and the shishya – disciple.

There is danger in using this style of teaching, for if the Guru who teaches what the student knows, then the student may feel that he knows it all and so why at all come to the guru. See the problem guru faces. I want you to understand that the guru also has a problem. If you tell the student what he already knows, he will say that he knows it all already. If the guru unfolds about what the student does not know, then the student will not understand as it would go over his head.

For example, earlier I told you one of the sutras – *I wun, wul ruk, e wong, hi ouch, haya varat, lun, jabakan gadakash, jabakada dash kapajathough, kapai shar hal...* How many of you understood it? I understood it because

I know the grammar sutras, but you don't, and so there
is no communication between us. So the Guru has to
start off with what the student knows, then leave aside
what the student knows, communicate something that
the guru knows, but in the process build a ladder
towards that state of knowing.

This type of classical teaching is called *Indu shaka nyaya*.
You want to know the Indu, the moon, you don't know
the moon; and so the guru says, "You know the tree, ah
ha, there is a tree, do you see that the tree has two
branches, ah ha, can you see the two big branches, yes,
now look in between the branches". And when the
student looks between the branches, he sees the moon.
That is why it is called *Indu shaka nyaya*.

I am saying this because you should know the classical
style of teaching. You teach your children in your own
style. In this style what you do is called *Adhyaropa
apavadha nyaya*. You say something – adhyaropa, – then
he negates it – apavadha. By saying something and
negating it, you are not catching the words. The essence
of the word is not the word, because the word is not the
thing and the description is not the described. The word
'water' is not water, the word 'biryani' is not briyani, but
the word is an indicator indicating the indicated, which
is other than the indicator.

I want you to understand the classical style of unfolding the sutras. If a person wants to listen to the classical teacher lecturing in the classical style, he must know that certain things will be said, certain things will not be said. This is because the teacher has to stimulate the process of thinking and the student has to start thinking about what the teacher is trying to convey.

"Some of us think, many of us think we think and most of us never think of thinking... The man of thinking is defined as one who knows to use the grand prerogative of the mind. Few think of thinking but many never think that they can think".

So the guru has to stimulate the process of thinking. So he will say something like, "I know well what I have said and what I have not said yesterday. He who is a thinking person will know the relation between what I have said and what I have not said." The mass is never a thinking group, but in the mass the guru is interested in the class. The person with classical bent of mind starts thinking, "Hey, guru said this, what is it that he is really going to say?" You start thinking and psychological collaterals of the understanding from the known to the unknown would be thus built. Psycho-logical collaterals from the known to the unknown, from the *vyakta* to *avyakta* would be built. And this style of teaching is called *adhyaropa apavadha nyaya*.

I want you to be sensitive to what I say. In between if
you get confused, be happy that you are confused. When
you get confused it means you can understand; buffalo
never get confused, it is the human being alone that gets
confused. Thinking requires that you get confused
initially.

For example, in the Brahma Sutra, written by Veda Vyasa,
there is a saying, "*Tattu Samanvayat*". This means that all
the Vedas ultimately speak the truth. Why does he say
this? Because at one place, the Veda says *Manasa evam idam
apthavyam* — "By the mind alone the truth is discovered";
in another place, it is written, *Yato vacho nivarthante aprapya
manasa saha* — meaning you have to go beyond the mind.

On the one hand the veda says that you have to go
beyond the mind and on the other, it says the mind alone
is enough. It appears there is a contradiction. One
portion of the Veda says *Tat srishtva tadevan pravashit* —
meaning that the Lord created the world; the other
portion of the Veda says *Neha nanasti kinchana* — there is
no creation at all. You see the contradiction. The
contradiction exists because the guru wants the student
to think. Hence, the great Saint Veda Vyasa, the author
of the most powerful text called Brahma Sutras, wrote
Tattu Samanvayat. It means there is *samanvayat*, which all
these scriptures are saying the same thing, it is not a
contradiction, it is not a paradox, it is not a dichotomy,

but there is a polarisation of dichotomy. In the process, guru makes you to think.

Earlier, I mentioned some things and did not elaborate on some things so that you start thinking. If not with your conscious mind, at least your subconscious mind would start thinking. I was unfolding on a particular verse even though I did not say the verse. I will unfold the sutra now.

7

Art of Creating a New Body

Shakti Sandhane Shareera Utpattihi.

This is a beautiful sutra taught by Lord Shiva to his consort Parvati. *Shakti sandhane*, O Parvati, when you are united to Shakti, *Shareera Utpattihi*, and a new body is created. Therefore, Lord Shiva emphasizes that this is not only the physical body but a new body is created. This physical body is *stula shareera* – gross body. We all think that we are this body. We find many ladies carry a mirror in their vanity bag and go on checking their face in the mirror, as if it disappears. They have to assure themselves that, yes, this is our face. People are under a great illusion and therefore a delusion that *Dhehe pushte aham pushtaha, dhehe nashte aham nashtaha.* When the body is strong, *aham pustaha* I am strong, *dhehe nashte,* when the body is destroyed, *aham nashtaha,* I am destroyed. So who am I? *Aham dhehaha,* I am the physical body.

But Lord Shiva says, "You are not seeing yourself, you are something more than the body, something which is *ateeta,* something which is beyond the body. Dhehe pushte aham pushtaha, dhehe nashte aham *nashtaha* – if you say you are only the body, when the body is destroyed, you are destroyed. When the body is born you are born, so you start with the body and end with the body. Not that you are not the body, but you are not *only* the body. This philosophy of thinking that you are only the body is a materialistic philosophy. No dharma can exist in such philosophy. There is no such thing as virtue – *punya,* no such thing as sin – paapa in such materialistic philosophy. Such a materialistic or atheistic philosophy is called "*Charvaka*" philosophy in the Indian culture.

I would like all of you to know little bit of Indian heritage. We have become so westernised. India has become India, not Bharat. Please understand the atheistic philosophy called *Charvaka.*

Charvaka says, "*Dehe pushte aham pushtaha, dehe nashte aham nashtaha*". Therefore, it is said, "*basmi bhoothasya dehaha kutaha aayatanam*". When the body, basmi bhoothasya, is destroyed, *kutaha aayatanam* – where will the new body come from? Therefore what you will do is *yaava jeeve sukam jeeve*, as long as you have to live, live happily.

But I have no money to live – it does not matter. *Rinam kritva gritham pibet* – you incur debt and eat a lot of ghee. You cannot pay the debt. So you say, *basmi bhoothasya dehaha kutaha aayatanam*, when the body is destroyed where is the question of coming back, and as you cannot come back, there is no *punya*, no *paapa*. So,"*yaava jeeva sukam jeeve*, rinam kritva gritham pibet".

In those days there was no cholesterol problem. Those days if one entered into debt, one had to clear it. But the follower of *charvaka* philosophy says, don't worry about that... once the body is destroyed you are not going to be reborn. Therefore, based on this shallow philosophy, which appears to be pseudo logical, no dharma can be created.

Lord Shiva dismantles the *charvaka* philosophy, the materialistic philosophy by saying that you are not just the *dheha*, you are not just a body, for there is something more than the body in you.

What is it that is something more than the body? It is called a *sukhshma shareeram*. *Stula shareeram, sukhshma shareeram* and the third body is called *kaarana shareeram*.

In Indian philosophy *stula shareeram* is the physical body, *sukhshma shareeram* is something *sukhshma*, something very subtle, and then there is *kaarana shareeram* or the 'causal body'. *Sukhshma shareera* is the 'aura body' – the energy field.

When the body dies, it is the *sukshma shareera* that goes from one birth to another birth. The physical body will not go. Every time you apply make-up to this body, it is on a shadow that you are applying the make-up. The real make-up has to be applied to the *sukhshma shareera* which consists of the *punya* - virtue that you acquire, and the *papa* – sin that you commit.

Once *prana* – life breath leaves the body, you are not going to take the body, not even one hair from your moustache, however decorative your moustache is. So a person who is a Shiva bhakta, a person who is a *dharmika* – follower of dharma takes care of the physical body as he understands that more than the body he is a *sukshma shareeram*. This *sukshma shareeram* and *kaarana shareeram* has to be discovered and experienced.

Shakthi Sandhane Shareera Utpattihi.

When you are united to Shakti, the *Iccha Shakti*, *Vidya Shakti*, *Kriya Shakti*... the three *shaktis* that you have and if you are living them, then you will have *shareera utpattihi*

— a new body is going to be born. This means you would discover the beautiful body called *sukshma shareeram*. Without being united to *shakti*, you would never discover it, you would never experience it.

What are these three *shaktis*? *Ichcha shakti* means the intention — all of us should have the intention that we are going to be enlightened. That is why *sanyas* is taken on Shivaratri. I too took *sanyas* on *Shivaratri*. Even if you are a V*aishnava* — Vishnu Bhakta, you will take *sanyas* on Shivaratri, because Lord Shiva represents destroying the ratri, the night or darkness in you. And how do you destroy the night inside you? What does Lord Shiva mean? *Mangalam. Sham mangalam karoti iti shiva.*

All of you, right now should have the *ichcha shakti* that you want to be enlightened. I told you India is more than geography, it is a vision. And the vision is *moksha -* enlightenment. That is why when a young boy initiated to *yagnopavita*, he wears a sacred thread with three strands. What do they stand for? The three strands in the sacred thread stand for the *Rig, Yajur* and *Sama Vedas…* that means the three Vedas would protect the wearer. The Vedas are the words of enlightened gurus. The words of enlightened gurus are the words of Lord Krishna, the words of Lord Shiva. These words should become your spiritual armour. *Rig, Yajur, Sama Vedas* are represented by three strands. In the three strands there is a knot called

'*Brahma granti*' which means that all the three Vedas ultimately unfolds Brahma Vidya.

Brahma means *moksha*, *Brahma* means *kaivalya*, *Brahma* means *nirvana*, Brahma means enlightenment. So the Vedas ultimately unfolds enlightenment. Your focus should be enlightenment and enlightenment alone.

Please understand that enlightenment should be your intention. Even marriage, ultimately leads to enlightenment. Before getting married you lived for yourself. The moment you get married the 'I' in you has to be divided into two. If you continue with only the 'I', your wife will finish you. The 'I' in you gets expanded to include the two of you or else you would become self-centred. From the union of two you get children.

It is said, *Aputrasya gatihi nasthi*. You must have *putra* — son. When you have *putra*, two becomes three. When the *putra* has another *putra*, then it becomes family tree. And so the 'I' in you continues to get expanded and diluted. Ultimately, when you get expanded and your hair turns grey, as Manu says, *grahastatu yada pashyet vali palittam atmanaha aptyasya cha apatyam tad aranyet samacharet*. That is, as the 'I' in you continues to expand, and when you turn sixty, or *grahastatu yada pashyet*, what happens next? *Vali palittam atmanaha* — your hair begins to grey; *aptyasya cha apatyam* when you become a grand father, *tad aranyet samacharet* – go to the forest and dedicate yourself full time in pursuit of enlightenment.

You cannot devote all your time to enlightenment if you are egocentric. So, dilute your ego. Or become a *sadhu*, which means that you should not live for yourself but you should live for the society.

So the 'I' in you again gets diluted. That is called 'selfless'... less of the self is called selfless. As of now, you are living with more of the self. When you get married it is less of the self, for there is you and your wife; when you get a child, there is also you, your wife, your child, your father-in-law and mother-in-law to consider. Before that, of course, there is you and your joint family.

Please understand the psychology, the philosophy, the metaphysics and the dynamics of them. The *Ichcha Shakti* - *ichcha* means enlightenment... *moksha*, nirvana should be the focus. Vidya Shakti – you should have clarity in life, not knowledge. *Kriya Shakti* is to know the distinction and to act on what you know. To know and not to act on what you know is equal to not knowing. Therefore, these three qualities - *Ichcha Shakti, Vidya Shakti, Kriya Shakti* – are important as *Shakti sandhane shareera utpattihi*.

Shakti sandhane, when you are united to *shakti* there is a

new *shareera, shareera utpattihi*. The new *shareera* is not the
one that you have created; but discovered. When you
discover you are not just the body, that there is
something beyond the body, a *sukshma shareeram* and you
start learning about the *sukshma shareeram* you would not
be limited to the body. The body would be a step for
you to go higher and you would begin to do and learn
something beyond the body.

In Zen philosophy, there is an expression – why does the
fish jump out of the ocean in between. The guru says
that the fish is exploring the world beyond the ocean.
There is something beyond the body; there is something
beyond the mind. Just don't limit yourself to the body.

In one of the Shiva Puranas, there is mention of a Shiva
bhakta, a Sadhu. His only mantra was *Om Namah Shivaya*.
For him, that became his food. Shiva says *Gnanam annam*.
That is, true understanding is *annam* for a wise person.
Eating food alone is not *annam*. *Gnanam*, that is, clarity
is *annam*. Once you know the joy of chanting the mantra,
the joy of *sankeertana*, the joy of *bhakti*, the joy of *vairaghya*,
that becomes *gnanam annam*... food for the soul.

When Shiva bhakta, a sadhu, a monk and an ascetic
chanted the mantra *Om Namah Shivaya*, it is said that
Lord Shiva Himself listened. Any true bhakta would
thus experience Lord Shiva. In what form Lord Shiva

presents Himself, He only knows. That is why it is said that even if you don't have eyes to see, you can see God in any form, in the form of a devotee or in the form of Bhakta.

In Ramayana Katha it is said that whenever you narrate the Ramayana, Hanuman is always seated in the crowd. It is a belief that if one narrates the Ramayana katha with great bhakti, Hanuman is to be found among the audience. Hanuman never develops *ahankara* – arrogance. God comes in all forms, in so many forms that even when the devotee out of sheer devotion chanting 'mara', God descended. So when the Shiva bhakta chanted the mantra *Om Namah Shivaya*, God descended and the bhakta began to chant the great mantra *Triyambhakam yajamahe* sugandhim pushtivardhanam uruvarukamiva *bhandanath mrityor mukshiya maamritat* – these are the two great mantras for Shiva bhaktas.

One is a Vedic mantra and the other is *panchakshari*. While a Bhakta was chanting out of devotion, he experienced the presence of God and felt very happy. He touched the feet of the Lord and said, "My Lord!" He was in a state of *vismayaha*... in a state of ecstasy, with tears flowing down. The Lord said, "You have chanted my name; now ask me what you want". The bhakta said, "I have seen you that is enough".

The Lord asked him, "Tell me what is that you want."
What does the devotee ask? "I don't want anything, O,
Lord. I have seen you and I don't want anything else. I
am filled." But the Lord asked again, "What do you
want?" The devotee said again, "I have seen you, I don't
want anything else" and then he turns and goes away
revelling in the memory, revelling in the *oorjha* of Lord
Shiva. Lord Shiva is not a vyakti, not a personality, but
an *oorjha*, an essence.

When the devotee turned to go away, the Lord said to
him, "My dharma is to give you" and the Bhakta said,
"By my dharma I have already received". So there is a
conflict between the bhakta and the Lord. The bhakta
is after all a sadhu and sadhus are not interested in
possessions. They give up everything, even the idea of
getting married.

Lord Shiva felt that it was his duty to give the bhakta
what he desired but the bhakta felt that to have the
Lord's darshan was enough. Finally the Lord blessed the
shadow of His bhakta, that wherever the shadow of the
Shiva bhakta went, it would spread peace, it would give
Shanti, Shanti, and Shanti. Therefore it is said, if you are a
Shiva bhakta you would not hanker for want, and even
if you do not bless another, whenever your shadow
touches somebody, the shadow would do the blessing.

Hence, very often we see that when a sadhu is invited somewhere, he may not bless those who are present, for he has no *ahankara* – arrogance to bless, but his *chaya* – his shadow, blesses the people.

Look at a tree – *chaayam anyasya kurvanti*. *Chayam* means shadow; the tree gives shade to others, but does not receive its own shade. "*Chayam anyasya kuruvanti swayam tishtanti atape*". It takes blazing heat of the sun and gives shade to others. *Phalani api parani ahuhu* – the tree does not take its fruit either, but gives it to others. So Shiva bhakta, the sadhu, is like a tree.

In the Shiva Purana it is said in beautiful verse that a *sambhashan* – a dialogue took place between Lord Shiva and His bhakta and therefore the shadow blesses wherever the devotee goes.

Why? Because his shadow has got *Ichcha Shakti*, *Vidya Shakti* and *Kriya Shakti*. When the three shaktis come together, the shaktis bring the oorjha... *sukshma shareera*. The *sukshma shareera*, which is calm and serene, does not require blessings. Therefore, wherever such a person goes, he spreads the 'energy field' for *shakti sandhane shareera utpattihi*. This is the whole sutra.

To sum up what I said Lord Shiva is seated on a tiger skin. The tiger has six important qualities. One is vision, which stands for focus. If you are a Shiva bhakta you should be focused. Right now you are listening to me and you should be focused; not only on my words but my gestures, not only on my gestures but my presence, the silence I am creating between the words. That is what you must focus on.

8

Transcending Activity
into Action

Let me narrate you a beautiful incident in the life of Akbar. Akbar records that the following incident changed his life greatly.

One day, when he was doing Namaz, a lady in a hurry touched him and went away searching for her beloved without even asking for apology. After the Namaz, Akbar found out who the lady was and summoned her and asked, "You know that I am the emperor, and yet, when I was praying, you touched me and went away without an apology." The lady who was a Sufi mystic said, "What kind of prayer is it, if you can feel my touch when you pray? I was searching for my beloved when I touched you accidentally and I did not even know that I touched you because I was so focused on my beloved. When you prayed to your beloved you could feel my touch; therefore your focus was not where it should have been, you were defocused."

If you watch a tiger when it is ready to attack its prey you will see how tremendously it is focused. If you and I are true Shiva bhaktas, we should also be tremendously focused. What should our focus be on? *Nirvana* – moksha. If your wife nags you, you are caught in the coils of *samsara*. Your focus should be how to convert the *samsara* into nirvana. If you are a Shiva bhakta, the *samsara* should become nirvana. That should be the focus.

Most of us worship the Lord but it is more a question of doing business with the Lord. You desire something and so you offer two coconuts and pray that God fulfills your desire, or maybe even two desires. Very few devotees are willing to drop their ego. When they worship God, they indulge in spiritual shopping. When you go to the mall you spend one thousand rupees to get something and when you go to a temple, you practice spiritual shopping.

A true Shiva bhakta is like a tiger that is focused. You should be focused similarly even while you are in difficulties. While you are experiencing difficulties... it could be that your husband may be dominating you, your wife may be nagging you, your boss may be scolding you, but your focus should be "Hey, this is the point for me to get enlightened."

Vyavasayātmika buddhirekeka kuru nandana
Bahu shākhā hyanantascha
Buddhayo' vyavasāyinam

Lord Krishna says, "*vyasaya atmika buddhihi*". When a drop of water falls on a hot pan, it becomes vapour. What happens when the same drop of water falls on a lotus leaf? It dances with joy, and reflects the sun or the moon. When the same dew drop falls into the oyster, it becomes a pearl.

Some of us are like the hot pan. Any amount of guru's *upadesha* or preaching we receive, it disappears. Some people are like the lotus. When guru says something, they receive the words like a dewdrop on the lotus leaf; but the moment external disturbance occurs, the dewdrop vanishes. The third type of people are like the oyster. Whatever they receive, they get pregnant with it and turn them into a pearl.

The Vedas say, "*Paunena shravanam kuryat*", you should listen constantly. In constant listening you understand. Of course, the understanding should click.

Surely, you have seen sometimes that when a joke is cracked, everybody laughs and you don't laugh because though you may understand the words spoken, you haven't really understood the point of the joke. Five days later when you are in the bathroom it clicks because everything gets released in the bathroom. Your ignorance also gets released there.

Hence the mantra *paunena shravanam kuryat* means *punaha punaha shravanam kuryat*. When I repeat what I said again and again I also added a lot of things. Like the tiger, remain focused and let your focus be on moksha.

What is the second quality of the tiger? Power. It has tremendous power. In life if you are truly a Shiva bhakta, you should have the power, the power of commitment. Without commitment, nothing is achieved. If you are a bhakta you should be tremendously committed to enlightenment.

The third quality of the tiger is commitment. One should have a commitment for enlightenment irrespective of any amount of distractions both internally and externally.

The fourth quality of the tiger is speed. You have to speedily practice spirituality right now; because death can happen any moment. *"Jatasya dhruvo mrtyuhu"*. All of you must understand this — "When you are born, *dhruvo mrtyuhu*", Lord Krishna says death is certain. Your horoscope may say that you may die after twenty years. But the astrologer who predicted may die much before. Any time you may die... so be extremely alert.

The fifth quality of the tiger is strategy. The tiger's strategy is about how to attack its enemy. One should develop a strategy to attack one's ignorance. Our core is ignorance. Everybody has core ignorance. One man's core ignorance could be sex. Another's core ignorance could be *moola Vidya* — root ignorance; a third may have anger as core ignorance, for another it may be power, name or fame. Develop a strategy to attack your ignorance.

The sixth quality of the tiger is skill. One should develop the skill to dismantle one's ego. "*Yogaha karmasu koushalam*", declares the Bhagavad Gita.

One should understand this from Lord Shiva.

Lord Shiva has also got a trishula — trident. What does the Trishula stand for? It stands for *sattva, rajas, tamas* — three gunas. The Bhagavad Gita unfolds three types of obstacles; the *sattvik* obstacle, the *rajasik* obstacle and the *tamasic* obstacle. First you should have *sattva* guna to get into *rajas* and *tamas*. Finally one has to have *sattva as*

predominant *guna*. Lord Shiva represents through *trishula*
— trident to remind us of the three gunas.

What are the three gunas? Sattva guna means very good
quality, but even that can be an obstacle. Even good
people suffer, and sometimes goodness itself becomes
an obstacle. For good people the biggest obstacle is their
image. I am a swamiji and I have a certain image. My
image itself is a big block. So we have to constantly learn
how to dismantle our image.

"Hiranmayena pātrena satyasyā mukham āpihitam",
declares Ishavasya Upanishad. *Hiranmayena pātrena* — with
golden disk, your image, *satyasyā mukhamāpihitam* — the
original face, *āpihitam* — it can cover. Please understand
that image plays a very, very strong role. *Sattva* can get
you over *rajas* and *tamas*, but *sattva* can also be an obstacle.
The Shiva Bhakta should hold a lot of obstacles like
Lord Shiva holds the trishula. The obstacles will be
there, but hold them up. And for good people, a good
image is very important but one should not get trapped
by a good image.

I do not exaggerate what I am saying. I have consciously
worked in my life to ensure that I don't build an image.
My students say that image building is very important.
As a guru, one has to build an image. I am not interested
in getting more people because of my image, but the

image influences people. Therefore I wear different clothes intentionally so that I am not hooked to an image.

Once when I was in the Himalayas, I met an old colleague. He had not come down from the Himalayas as he had chosen to stay there. He told me that by opening a trust I have got into samsara. He told me that after studying in the ashram he had decided against samsara and he is in a state of nirvana. He said, "You have set up a trust and now you go after trustees and salaam them and blah, blah, blah, blah." He went on talking in this manner. I listened quietly and asked him if he were free. He said, "Yes, I am free, for I have no samsara."

Another time, we were at Rishikesh. I was wearing a red tracksuit and I was about to go trekking. This colleague told me, "I have an extra pair of slippers, please wear them with your *angavasthra* – a loose cloth wrapped around and we will go trekking." I told him that a red tracksuit fits the sadhu and that instead of slippers, I can offer him a nice pair of shoes that are also red in colour. He was a very sweet sadhu and he felt that he could not wear a red tracksuit. Then he realised that though he thought he was free, he was not really free. So I say the real dropping is inward, not the outward dropping.

Thus we get stuck with the image that is there with us. So the first thing to do is to drop the image of who we are. Just be empty. It is true that when we have to live in society we have to have some image; but it is important that you are master of your image and not a victim of your image. I should have the image of a sadhu but I should not let my image rule me. There has to be a very delicate balance between the image and you. In worldly life you need to have an image but you should not be imprisoned by the image. Therefore there are two *bhandanas* — bondages mentioned in the Bhagvad Gita - one is image and the other is *gnana bhandana*, which means that you are stuck to your own knowledge. It is called the *sattva* obstacle but I will not dwell on this now.

The second guna is *rajo guna*. You should be master of the *rajo guna* too. What is rajo? Rajo means activity. There is a difference between action and activity. Action is something we have to do, but activity is an obstacle. Activity is mechanical.

Most of us think we are performing an action but actually, we are lost in activity. Most of us act to cover our inner void. That is why you cannot sit down in one place and remain quiet. When you sit down doing nothing, you say, "I am bored, Swamiji." Why are you bored? Because of the well of boredom within you. What do you do when you get bored? You switch on the TV

— not because you are interested in the programmes, but to cover up your inner void. How often you pick up the phone and call a friend and say, "How are you", not because you are concerned about the other person but because you are bored with yourself and you seek to fill the void. Actually our actions are an escape from our own self. "Isn't the weather hot?" you tell someone when you meet them; the weather is only an excuse. An excuse to escape from yourself. Such an action which we indulge in to escape from ourself, to avoid ourself, is called activity.

Buddha gave us some wonderful advice to handle this — *Abhi Mukhi*. Encounter your inner void, encounter your shallowness, encounter your emptiness, encounter the ways you use to escape, through a conversation, or through an activity. Don't develop yet another escape route. Encounter yourself.

What is this inner void? Am I really the void? *Abhi Mukhi* - face it. Encounter it. Once you face it and encounter it you understand that you are escaping from yourself for two reasons. I pause for you to dip in the Ganga of activities. We use activity as a form of escape for two reasons. They are fear and greed. You look at your activities - you may be very busy, you may be running a hospital, you may be running ashrams — if it is action, no problem, but if it is activity it is a form of escape.

And what is it that we escape through activity?

Even when you indulge in social service or charitable activities it is all a means of escape, because inside yourself, you are bored, you are shallow. Why are you shallow? Because your perception of yourself is so distorted and not based on facts. You justify and console yourselves in social activities.

When you do social service, let it be an action and not an activity. In all our activities we should follow the words of Buddha and practice *abhi mukhi*. Encounter yourself and see what lies behind your actions, even a discourse like this. If I am not sensitive and not cognizant, if I talk because I am bored and somebody has to talk, then even my discourse can become a mere activity. Lord Shiva refers to *abhi mukhi* as *Chaitanya Atma*. *Chaitanya* means awareness; if you see yourself with awareness, not the *outer* self, but the *inner* self, then you will see that behind your activity there is either fear or greed.

Years ago, when I was hardly 26 - 27 years old, I was interviewed by Channel 9, a very famous Australian channel. I remember the lady who was interviewing me asked, "Can you tell in a nutshell what kind of stress people are going through?" Based on the great teachings of many masters, I said the stress people go through is, "the greed to become somebody and the fear of being nobody".

This is the greatest stress people are going through even today.

Have you observed the greed people have to become somebody? Many people come and ask me, "Swamiji, you are a good speaker, your books are all best sellers but why do you have only one ashram? That other guru who cannot even speak well has twenty four ashrams. He talks in commas, not even in sentences." So you see, there is greed everywhere. Really, the greed to become somebody and the fear of being nobody is the greatest stress.

Lord Buddha says that greed and fear seem to be the mother of all our activities. Have you studied greed? Greed is a symptom of shallowness. Fear is a symptom of shallowness and in that shallowness we have to discover a way out.

Everywhere there is greed, and more greed. In my corporate workshops, I tell them that in this rat race, even if you win you continue to be a rat. You are a multi millionaire and feel that the other company is better than your company. And you become tense. In all my workshops, I have people saying, "Their turnover is much more, Swamiji, motivate our employees to increase the turnover." And afterwards what do you do? You find another ladder to climb.

I am not against progress. I am saying the very context of this progress is an escape route from your inner void.

Let me tell you a story.

 Mullah Nasruddin wanted to get married. In his town there were many rich sheikhs. His friend advised him not to consider beauty, for beauty is only skin-deep, and instead to find a rich man and marry his daughter. The Mullah, who was a handsome guy, found out that the richest person was Sheikh Abdulla. He went to him and told him he wanted to get married to his daughter. Sheikh Abdulla asked him which daughter he wished to marry, for, he said, he had a battalion of daughters, "My youngest daughter is 20 years old, if you marry her, I will give you 5 lakh rupees. Another daughter is 25 years old, if you marry her I will give you 20 lakh rupees. A third daughter is 40 years old, if you marry her I will give you 40 lakh rupees. A fourth is 48 years old and if you marry her I will give you I crore rupees. Mullah Nasruddin asked the Sheikh if he had a daughter who was 65 years old. See the greed of the man. When the Sheikh replied in the negative, the Mullah asked, "Who is the lady next to you? I will marry her". She was Sheikh Abdulla's wife. "Well, I don't mind marrying her. So long as the amount increases, it is Ok". What is this greed?

Do you remember Mahatma Gandhi's statement that there is enough in this world for man's need, but not for his greed?

When you earn wealth, do so not out of greed but for the joy of earning. In the Artha Shastra, Kautilya says that one must earn money but not out of greed. Greed, he says, is like a pot with a hole; all the water you pour into it will flow out. He says that your mind is like a pot, and when you have greed it is a hole in the pot. In such a space, even the blessings of God will not stay with you but will simply go away. So, says Kautilya, we should earn money out of love and not out of greed.

The moment you earn to validate yourself, you are earning to cover up your inner void. Have you seen how when some people suddenly become rich, they wear a number of gold rings everywhere? I have a relative who became rich suddenly when land prices shot up; he wore a gold watch and every time you see him, he will raise his hand to show off his gold watch.

Your rajasik obstacle is thus an activity you undertake to avoid yourself. It is not action; action is important –

"na hi kaschit kshanamapi jātu tishkatya karmakrt". Lord
Krishna says nobody can remain without action. This is
why, in a Buddhist country, even a married man becomes
a monk for one month every year. You do this for you
have to face yourself. Afterwards, you can wear the
saffron dress, and then remove it so on. This is because
of the emphasis Buddha laid on *abhi mukhi*, his famous
teaching.

Please understand your activity and face it. You will
always see the greed and fear. A lot of people get married
out of fear that they may be lonely otherwise, but there
is no guarantee that your wife lives or stays with you,
no guarantee at all. Somebody asked if there is any
guarantee after marriage. None. Especially with marriage,
there is no guarantee. Yet people always act out of fear.
Out of fear people get married. Out of fear they have
children. What if your son goes away to America?
Encounter your fear first.

Lord Shiva holding the trishula is highly symbolic. It
means he is holding the action within him, his action is
not running out of fear, his action is not running out
of greed. Please understand and look within yourself. If
you are a Shiva bhakta, chanting *Om Namah Shivaya* is not
enough; you have to understand the fear within you, you
have to look at your fear with *Chaitanya atma*.

9

Fear to Fearlessness

What is fear ultimately? Fear exists in comparison. Only when you start comparing do you feel afraid. Why should one compare? After all, if I eat some food, your stomach, your *'madhya pradesh'* will not fill up. You may say, "Oh Swamiji, without comparison how can we live?" I tell you, you can live. Compare but don't whip yourself with your comparisons, inspire yourself through comparison. If somebody is wearing beautiful diamond earrings, you look at them and curse your husband. You wonder why you married this *bhakasura*, for although you prepare chicken for him whenever he wants it, you are wearing ordinary earrings while this person is wearing diamond rings. You complain to your husband and your husband says that you should be happy that at least you have ears. You ask him to buy you diamond earrings for you are so miserable because of someone else's diamond earrings. This comparison is whipping you, torturing you, stigmatizing, victimizing, ravaging and bulldozing you. You should be able to stop such comparisons. When somebody wears diamond earrings, you should be able to admire them without wanting to possess them. Actually, if you see the movie *Blood Diamond*, you may never wear a diamond anymore. The way diamonds are procured has become such a crime.

Lord Shiva in his *Vignyana bhairava tantra* gave Parvati 112 techniques of meditation, and said that when you look at somebody, don't make a comparison that kills you, but compare in a way that inspires you. Lord Shiva says that when you look at somebody, look with a fresh perspective, as though you are seeing that person for the first time. If God appears in front of you, how will you look at him? You look with a sense of wonder.

Similarly, when you look at someone, don't get polluted by your past or by your future. Don't get pulled by your likes and your dislikes. When you look at somebody with a fresh perspective, look at the person with a deep sense of wonder; look as though you are seeing this person for the first time. Lord Shiva says in his sutra that when you do this, you will experience — *"poorna madah, poornamidam, poornāt poornamudacchate, poornasya poornamādāya poornamevāvshishyate".* He says that you will experience poorna, the sense of poorna — *poorna madah* that is *poornam, poornamidham.*

And when that happens, you should also practice this beautiful sutra, *Vismayaha yogabhoomika. Yoga* means spiritual, *bhoomika* means foundation; *yoga bhoomika* means the foundation of your spiritual life and *vismayaha* means wonderment. The foundation of your spiritual life should be *vismayaha*, wonderment. Rabindranath Tagore saw the dewdrops on the lotus leaf and poetry came out. The gross person sees the Niagara Falls and thinks gross thoughts of diarrohea and dysentery.

The Lord says, *"Vismayaha Yogabhoomika"*. Lord Shiva puts the *naamam* that is called *Vibhuti*, holy ash. Every devotee has to understand that the body has to become vibhuti. You have to remind yourself that the body is going to be vibhuti and not invest everything in the body. There is something beyond the body; respect the body and treat it well, but ultimately it is going to become vibhuti. Let the very foundation of your spiritual life be *Vismayaha -* wonderment.

When does that state of wonderment happen?

The Vignana Bhairava Tantra, a famous text, says when

you look at the moon, look as though you are seeing the moon for the first and only time; look with totality, with intensity and suddenly a *Vismayaha* happens to you. Then you will experience the fullness. You are listening right now listen as though you are listening for the first time.

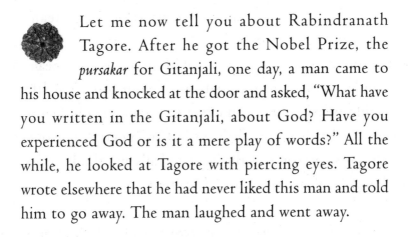 Let me now tell you about Rabindranath Tagore. After he got the Nobel Prize, the *pursakar* for Gitanjali, one day, a man came to his house and knocked at the door and asked, "What have you written in the Gitanjali, about God? Have you experienced God or is it a mere play of words?" All the while, he looked at Tagore with piercing eyes. Tagore wrote elsewhere that he had never liked this man and told him to go away. The man laughed and went away.

That night, Tagore could not sleep. The next day when he went for a walk, and was reflecting on what the man had said, he saw some birds flying. He knew then that when he wrote Gitanjali, he did not experience the birds; he had experienced the poetry of the words, which was really magical, but the real thing – the birds flying, the gentle breeze associated with it, the sun reflected in the water, the buffaloes which were swimming in the water but appeared to be dancing in the rippling water – had been beyond his experience. Tagore understood now that the sun was magical, the breeze was magical, the birds and butterflies were magical, and then he found that the sun was reflected in the lake although the buffaloes were dirtying the water. The experience of this wonder then flashed on Tagore, that the sun remains uncontaminated in spite of the dirty water. The sun is magical and when reflected in the water, it remained unaffected and uncontaminated.

Therefore in the dirt, he could see the beauty, and he could have the aesthetic experience of oneness in the sun; he saw beauty in the sun, beauty in the buffalo, beauty in the dirty water, the beauty of the sun reflected on the water, and the beauty of the sun not contaminated by the dirty water.

After that great experience, Tagore rushed to meet the man who he had spoken to the previous day. Tagore wrote that though he had disliked the man earlier, he now found that his eyes held a peaceful look, not a piercing gaze. And that man told him, "I know you have experienced God." The man's eyes now appeared gentle, soothing, beautiful and all-embracing. You see, when Tagore saw the man that day, he saw him with totality, with a fresh perspective. Please understand that when you experience something, you should be available to that experience like Rabindranath Tagore was. Vignana Bhairava Tantra says that when you look at the sun, look as though you are seeing it for the first time. When a lover looks at his beloved, he says, "Wah!" but when the same beloved becomes a wife, he stops seeing his wife afresh.

Therefore, friends, comparison is not the problem, at the same time comparison is the problem. I may appear to contradict myself. What type of comparison can you make when fear exists in comparison? When you see somebody more beautiful than you, instead of fearing comparison, fine-tune it, purify comparison, sanctify it, baptise it, transform the comparison.

Rabindranath Tagore saw beauty in the sun, saw beauty in the dirty water, saw beauty in the sun reflected on the water, and saw that the sun was not polluted by the dirty water and then, *vismayaha yoga bhoomika*. There was *vismayaha*, a sense of wonderment, a sense of 'Wah!' a sense of ecstasy, a sense of *oorjha* dancing in a forgotten language called bliss. That is why the word ecstasy means beyond your self.

When you are listening to me right now listen as though this is your first time. You know, I love dogs. When I said this somewhere else, one person was shocked that being a Swamiji, I could love dogs. I replied in jest, "Oh, I love so many things including you." It is very dange-rous to be with a sadhu. That is why they say that sadhu is like fire. If you come too close you may get burnt. If you are too far away you may never get the warmth. So, you decide where you want to be.

To compare like this is hell, so next time don't compare, just look and see afresh. *Vismayaha* – once you see *vismayaha*, everything becomes *yoga bhoomika*. So comparison is not the problem. If you can bring, like Rabindranath Tagore, a fresh perspective to every moment, then you will experience – *poornamadaha poornamidam poornāt poornamudacchāte* – every moment is full and complete.

The second type of fear exists in a relationship. *Rajas* acts in fear. I told you *rajas* is an activity – an activity that has either greed or fear behind it.

Have you seen that relationships also have a lot of fear and the fear is actually just a movement of thought? When fear is a movement of thought that thought in a relationship causes people to say, "Swamiji, I am afraid I may lose my wife. I am afraid I may lose my husband." I tell them that you are afraid you will lose your husband or wife, because you have the image of your husband; you have the image of your wife. They feel disappointed and say that I am not relating to the husband or the wife. I tell them, "You are relating to your impression of your husband, to your impression of your wife. Therefore you never relate to a person. You relate to the imprint you make on the other person." Don't you think it is right?

So if you want to drop that fear, I just want you to connect to that person and that thought with his images to come. Connect your thought with the impressions that are going to come; connect your thought with the structures that are going to come; connect your thought with that imagery dynamics that are going to come and if you can pierce through all those images, look at your guru as a guru. Zen philosophy says a rose is a rose is a rose is a rose.

Your wife is your wife, but you don't see your wife. Instead, you form an impression and that impression becomes memory. Now, memory is the representation of the past, and you must remember that your wife is not the past; your wife is the present. You relate your present from the past. You relate your present from your memory. You are struggling with your memory of your wife. You are not seeing the flow or the glowing being. It requires a lot of control. You can drop the impression and see a person as a person for as Zen philosophy says, a rose is a rose is a rose.

The *Vignana Bhairava* Tantra reminds you that when you look at a flower, you should see the flower as if it were the first time you see it. Don't bring in the past or the future, just look at it and then a sense of exuberance, an ecstasy, a dance, a miracle happens in your perception. This heightened perception gives you the experience of "Wah!" When that happens, even if you go away to the bathroom, the state of heightened perception continues.

Therefore you have to see with *chaitanya atma*. Your *atma* should be full of awareness not with the garbage of words. When you relate to a person, see the person as a person. Fear will cease to exist. In the absence of fear, there won't be activity; there will be action and you should be able to control *rajas*.

Your activity comes from greed and fear. Observe the fear. What is this fear that people have? Fear is a movement from certainty to uncertainty. Just observe. Pause. Feel. Don't capture my understanding through the structure of words. Capture my understanding through my presence and through the essence of the words. Only then will you create words that are not an imitation of what I say. All shisyas, as you have seen, copy the guru.

Fear is a movement from certainty to uncertainty. What happens to your imprint? What happens to your psychological software of understanding? You will say, "Uncertainty should not exist in my life. I want my life to be a movement from certainty to certainty to certainty." Then your title will be 'PhD Among Fools'. If you look into people's software of understanding, which is in the hardware of the brain, they want everything to be certain. They ask, "What is the guarantee, Swamiji, that if I marry this person, he will stay with me?" What guarantee? There is no guarantee. Then why do people get married? Because they learn to enjoy uncertainty. Then why I am not married, you may ask me and that's because I am very uncertain.

I sometimes confuse people, it's because I am unpredictable. I am unpredictable because I give unexpected examples. When I become unpredictable they want me to be predictable. They want me to be certain, but I am uncertain. And if any matured souls are there in the audiences they may feel "My God, what fun it is, Swamiji is unpredictable". You see any possibility is possible. So you are in thrill I am in thrill, life is such a thrill. I am saying there is a craze, there is addiction towards certainty. Can you drop that?

"*Jagat jayate gachchati iti jagat*". As you know, the word *Jagat* means world; *jayate* means the world is born, *gachchati* means it goes, that is, the world is changing. As you know, any change is uncertain; when the world around us would change we do not know. The world is changing and we want to be certain how to relate to the change. This causes us to create a conflict with the world. It is not possible to swim in the water without getting wet. Similarly, when the world is changing it means there is uncertainty and by wanting the world to be certain, we

are creating a conflict. Listen carefully. When you create
conflict you say life is tortuous. Life is not tortuous.
Your expectation of life is hyper-stupidity.

Therefore, *"Bhajagovindam Bhajagovindam Bhajagovindam
Govindam bhaja moodamathe"*. Adi Shankaracharya says
mooda mooda mooda — The word *mooda* — fool is full of love
for me. Even though the world is changing we don't want
it to change. The river is flowing but we don't want the
river to flow, we want it to be a lake. Instead of flowing
with the river, we want the river to be a lake and we are
angry at the river because it is moving.

Fear is a movement from certainty to uncertainty.

Actually, if you see clearly, every movement is from
uncertainty to uncertainty to uncertainty and every uncertainty is a surprise, because you don't know anything
about the next moment. The moment you don't know,
it is a surprise and the surprise may be beautiful or
horrible. It is like going to a movie and you don't know
the ending of the movie. A movie is interesting because
you don't know how it will end. Life is beautiful because
you don't know.

But your software makes you want to know everything.
This is why every horoscope reader will exploit you
because he feels he knows you, although he himself does

not know and that is why the horoscope has become a 'horrorscope'. Why the very craze for horoscopes to foretell your future? You want life to be predictable. The craze for cosmetics and the growth of the cosmetics industry, which is next to the missile industry, shows that you can't accept your body. God has given you pale lips, so you want red lips. When you have red lips, you want them to be purple. All these are symptoms that you cannot accept yourself. So too, understand the fact that you are crazy about your future... you do not know how to live in the present.

Let me tell you a simple thing – life is unpredictable and it is wonderful that life is unpredictable. It is wonderful that life is uncertain. It is a 'Wah!' experience that you don't know what life is going to be the next moment. Since you don't know every moment, you look for what you don't know, 'Wah!' you start dating with the new. Dating is always more interesting than marriage. When you are dating someone, you don't take your partner for granted. Dating is very interesting because you don't know whether it is going to be a 'Yes' or a 'No'. And not knowing is such a thrill. When Leila was waiting for Majnu, it is said that even when a leaf moved she thought, "I think Majnu is coming" and Majnu thought, "Leila is coming". If you don't have that experience, then your life is going to be miserable.

That is why in my book I have given this story:

A man went to a mental hospital on his anniversary to distribute sweets to the inmates.

There he saw a patient holding on to the window and shouting 'Leila, Leila, Leila'. He asked the warden for the reason and was told that the man's Leila had run away, his beloved had run away. He had become imbalanced and he still expected that she would return. The visitor went to another room. There too, there was another person shouting 'Leila, Leila, Leila'. He asked the warden what had happened to that person. The warden told him that the second patient had become mad because he married that Leila.

Honestly, I am telling you, anyone can land up in this madness. I am giving you the experience of many *janmas* – births; that is why in this janma, I am not married.

If you look at your husband or wife with absolute freshness, and one day your wife nags you, it will be so beautiful. Today somebody was giving me a Thai massage, a 2½ hour massage. They twisted my arms and it was painful but also a pleasure. Every moment you see, there is uncertainty and uncertainty is beautiful. Please stop thinking that uncertainty is a crime. Stop thinking of uncertainty as a curse. Stop this craze to be certain. Then, you experience *vismayaha yoga bhoomika*.

The Ordinary Eye
to the Eye of Intuition

The Trishula stands for sattva, rajas and tamas. If your activity is greed and fear, drop it and then you will be master of yourself. After sattva and rajas, the third quality is Tamas. Tamas means indolence. The greatest laziness is that we never ask who we are. You cannot understand the words who am I? In my LIFE and Management workshops, I tell them that if you cannot understand, "Who is in"? Then, "Are you in"? If you cannot understand that, God bless you. Ask yourself who is inside you; ask yourself what are your thoughts. Are you into the magic of your thoughts? Are you available to the magic of your emotions? Are you available to the magic of feelings? Are you available to the dance of your likes and dislikes, your kama, your krodha, your lobha, your mada, or your matsarya? If you are available to the magic and dance, then "Yatra yatra mano yati, tatra tatra samadhayaha". It says that for such a person who is into the magic of life, into the magic of movement of up and down, *yatra yatra mano yati* let the mind go anywhere, *tatra tatra samadayaha* he is in the state of *Samadhi*. But our greatest laziness is that we never ask, "Who is in".

So when the trishula is held thus, it means that *sattva*, *rajas* and *tamas* should be in your control, and then you are a Shiva bhakta – devotee. When Lord Shiva is seated on the tiger skin, six qualities – vision, power, commitment, speed, strategy and skill are to be learnt which have been explained earlier. The vibhuti reminds us that ultimately the body is going to be reduced to ashes. When Lord Shiva's third eye opens, it reminds men and women not to look at life with ordinary eyes, but to look at life with Shiva's third eye, called the intuitive eye. Look at life from the eye of intuition.

If you read the life of Edgar Cayce, one of the greatest healers in American history, you will find that he was arrested because he used to heal people; he would go into a trance and prescribe medicines. In America one cannot do this if you are not a certified doctor. But Edgar Cayce's medicine worked. He was the best healer. Later, the Edgar Cayce Foundation was set up; he also made unbelievable predictions. It is said whenever Edgar Cayce went into a trance and made his predictions, both his eyes were focused in between the eyebrows which is called as third eye. His eyes are turned towards the third eye. This has been documented.

Ramanujam, the great mathematician, used to solve in one day problems that took great mathematicians six months to one year time. Whenever Ramanujam, the great mathematician from India solved a problem, it is said, his eyes were focused between the eyebrows.

Two cases of great giants show the working of the intuitive eye. The study of the brain has shown that the D quadrant of the brain has intuition. So look at life not from the ordinary eye, but from the eye of intuition. The ordinary eye sees only matter. The scientist's eye sees electrons, protons and neutrons going at tremendous speed. Science does not call it matter but energy in motion. There is a lot of space in matter; science fiction says if you take away the space even the huge concert hall can be put in a matchbox. It can be done in science fiction.

Therefore, the great saints, great enlightened masters and great rishis have said that we must look at life not with the ordinary eye, but the third eye, the eye of intuition.

Therefore Lord Shiva has the third eye, and Hindus put
the *bindu* or the *naama* in between the eye brows; it means
that one should look at life from the eye of an enlightened master, from the eyes of wise people.

We say, '*Avahanam samarpayami, asanam* samarpayami,
padayoho padyam samarpayami, *argyam samarpayami...*
Avahanam means to invoke or call these qualities. Next
time when you worship Lord Shiva these qualities should
be *avahanam* – invoked. Then, you are a Shiva bhakta and
you know that Lord Shiva is not a personality, he is an
experience. Lord Shiva is a vision. Hence we say, '*Sham
mangalam karoti iti shivaha*'. Why *mangalam karoti*, because
vismayaha yoga bhoomika. Every moment is *vismayaha.*

"*Shakti sandhane shareera utpattihi*". When you are united
with *shakti* there is a new *shareera* born; with the new
shareera you look at the world as *gnanam annam.* This
understanding let you understand that *gnanam* is *annam*
and that is possible with *chaitanya atma*, when your *atma*
is full of *chaitanyas.*

Next, we will dwell on the sutra, "*Atma Nartakaha*". How
your *atma* – self is going to be a dancer dancing in
ecstasy.

11

We Attract both
Good and Bad

"What should I do in order to be enlightened?" asked the student to the master.

The master said, "Do as much as you can do to make the sun rise and the sun set."

Means what? Nothing.

"Then what is the use of all the spiritual practices?" enquired the student.

"To make sure that you are awake when the sun rises and the sun sets", said the master.

Most of us are not awake to the magic of life. Most of us are not awake to the blessings of life. Saint Kabir said when people say that they are unhappy, it is like the fish in the ocean saying that it is thirsty. It is thirsty for it does not know how to open its mouth. So too, if we are not awake, we cannot say we are filled with the ocean of blessings of the Lord for we are not able to receive it.

All spiritual practices, be it a Vaishnava practice, be it a Shaiva practice, be it a Vedantic practice, it is only to make sure you are awake, your receptors are awake to see the magic, the miracle, the dance, the ecstasy, the poetry, and the benediction of life.

I told you the story of Lord Shiva blessing the shadow of the bhakta. In the Shiva Purana there is another beautiful story, and it goes as follows:

There was a great Shiva bhakta. His only *annam*-food was the *uchcharanaam* — utterance of Lord Shiva's name. In the Shiva sutra there is a sutra which says, "*Gnanam annam*". The real *annam* is under-standing. Understanding is *gnanam* — wisdom, *bhakti* — devotion and *vairaghya - detachment*. Even though Shiva tells Parvathi *gnanam annam*, true gnana is clarity, bhakti and vairaghya. That is why when you perform a pooja, the priest makes you do *sankalpa - commitment*, "*gnana bhakti vairaghya siddhyartham aham idam poojayam karishye*". To increase your *gnan*, to increase your *bhakti*, to increase your *vairaghya*, to attain these siddhis – accomplishments (siddhyartham), I (*aham*) this (idam) am performing this pooja (poojyam karishye).

Whatever pooja you perform, the *sankalpa* – the stand that you take is to increase your clarity of life, to increase your bhakti and to increase vairaghya. Vairaghya means sense of detachment. When you don't develop *vairaghya* in your life, when you have to leave your wife, when you have to leave your children, the toughest part would be to leave your body also. There are some people who are so attached to the body that when they die, they cannot leave the body and try to stay on, like a ghost.

Therefore, the *shraddha* – rites after death you do is to tell the soul to not get attached to the body or the family and to leave on its journey when it is time.

That is why in *yogasana*, after doing all the *asanas* - postures to take care of the wonderful body of the Lord, what do you do at the end? You do the *Shavasana*. *Shava* means the sheer body lying like a dead body – the *asana* reminds us that ultimately we are going to die. So we should develop *vairaghya* – detachment.

So, the Shiva bhakta of our story had practiced this sutra of Lord Shiva – *gnanam annam*. Gnanam includes gnanam, bhakti and vairaghya, and he was doing all these only through the *uchcharanam* – utterances of Om Namah Shivaya and the Mritunjaya Mantra. He would chant these two *mantras*. In that region where he lived whenever it did not rain, they used to call this Shiva bhakta, this monk, this ascetic would go to that village sit down and chant the mantra. Not loudly but silently. And invariably it rained. Once it rained it seems he would get up and go away. He did not wish to get attached to the place. It is called *parivrajaha* – not to get attached to any place. So whenever famine threatened, the people would call this Shiva bhakta.

In the Shiva purana it is said that one day, when he was called to a village, he went and sat down, closed his eyes and chanted the mantra silently. The people did not even realize he was chanting the mantra inwardly when suddenly it began to rain. One youngster touched his feet and asked, "What is your magic? How do you cause this miracle to happen, for wherever you go it rains?" He replied, "It is not me." "Then who is it?" The bhakta – devotee said, "When I sit down, I do just one thing; with great bhakti, with deep belief in Lord Shiva, I harmonise myself and I chant the mantra." When he chanted the mantra, more than the mantra, he created an internal harmony within himself, an inner ecological balance within himself. Nature always exists in harmony with the person who is in harmony. The bhakta – devotee was in harmony and so nature was in harmony and therefore blessings, *parjanyaha* – rain, poured down.

Please feel this story.

In this story it reflects that if you are in harmony, then nature is going to be in harmony. If you are in conflict, then nature is in conflict. Like the saying, birds of a feather flock together. We attract situations in life. Therefore esoteric teaching tells us that all the wars you see outside are all because of the wars within ourselves. All the external wars are wars within us. When there are wars within ourselves, every thought which creates a war within, generates an energy pocket of violence. The micro contributes to the macro and the macro is filled with violence. The micro supports the macro and the macro supports the micro. The reverse also takes place. When there is a war outside, basically there is a war inside within us. Our individual micro level jumps to macro level through violence. And therefore we attract war. It is one of the important teachings of esoteric teachings.

We attract wars, we attract violence. And therefore if we decode the story in the Shiva purana, we find that if we are in harmony, every harmonious thought creates an energy pocket of harmony; so the micro generates the macro and when the micro generates macro nature is in harmony with us. And therefore the benediction of rain in the form of blessings takes place. Please digest this.

The bhakta – devotee said that more than the mantra, the beauty is in the harmony that we create. We are only an instrument for that inner harmony. That is why whenever mass violence takes place, the mass mind or the mass psychology takes over the individual mind. If the whole place is full of violence, even a person who is non-violent and is in that crowd of violence, you will find that suddenly he has also become very violent. The violence in the crowd creates a violent pocket all around and the macro mind will dominate the micro mind and the micro mind gets converted to the mode of the macro mind. Therefore in a situation of violence mass psychology takes over individual psychology.

That is why when a *japa* or *havan* is performed and there is chanting of mantras, all the energies that are generated get into the macro level and the result is harmony. This is how we attract situations in life.

In my LIFE workshop I always talk on this concept, that we attract situations in life. A drunkard will attract a drunkard. When a drunkard goes to a temple, he meets someone who is a drunkard. At my LIFE workshop we have a break after a two hour session; I ask people to mix around and I find that invariably unhappy looking people look out for unhappy looking people in the crowd. And both share notes and say, "Swamiji tells us to be happy; let him get married to my wife then we will see how happy he is." Happy looking people look out for happy looking people and both exchange notes. Drug addicts always attract drug addicts. In fact it appears that they have receptors or radar to find people who are to their liking.

So, be in harmony. You can chant any mantra to be in harmony but merely chanting the mantra mechanically is not going to help.

Many years ago, when I was in Mysore, I used to go to a house for food. I was hardly 24 years then. My mother also stayed in the house at times. One day, the lady of the house told me, "Swamiji, every day I do 50 malas of japa for you, 200 malas of japa for my husband and 150 malas of japa for my mother in law." I wondered where she got time for so many malas of japa." It was after all a joint family. Later, my mother who was staying there told me how the japa was done. The lady says *Ommmmmm Namah Shivayaaaaaaaa*, and the whole japa mala was over.

If you do like this, the japa mala may be smoothened but you will remain rough. People sometimes tell me that they have gone through the whole Bhagavad Gita but

nothing has happened to them. You may have gone
through the Bhagavad Gita but the question is whether
the Bhagavad Gita has gone through you.

Please digest this story from the Shiva Purana that I have
told you. Be in harmony, for once you are in harmony
mysterious things happen. If you ask anybody doing
good work how help can come from unknown sources,
they will tell you that initially there may be difficulties,
but help will arrive. I am talking out of experience but
if you ask other people, they will say the same thing.

Please understand what Lord Shiva represents; take those
qualities of Lord Shiva with the sutras I have told you
and keep yourself in harmony. You may go through some
external famine but nature will support you and be in
harmony with you. We all go through difficulties.
Problems are inevitable in life but suffering is optional.

The Mystery of Karmic Principle

This brings us to another story. All these stories can be found in the puranas. I have modified some of them to narrate in my book called LIFE.

This story is about a man who did not believe in God, an atheist. Later he became a great Shiva bhakta. The story goes that though he did not believe in God, one day, God descended into his being. A divine light appeared in front of him and said, "I am Tryambakeshwara – Lord Shiva". The man thought to himself, "I have never done Shiva japa, never done Shiva upasana, never been to a temple, never been a believer in God and yet Shiva appears to me in the form of a light and asks me to do a seva – service."

Now the light was mystical, the light was extremely esoteric and it said, "I want you do me a favour". And this man, though he was not a believer, said, "Yes, I will. What do you want me to do?"

The divine light said, "There is a rock outside your house. It is a huge rock and is on the edge of the cliff. I want you to push it."

This man was not a believer, and wondered why God had asked him to perform this task for he just could not understand it. Suddenly, he was filled with mystic energy and he realised that the ways of the Lord are beyond logic. He said, "Yes, I will do it". His experience made him believe and so he agreed. The Vedas say 'Na tarkena apaniya' – there are some things that you will not understand by using logic; you have to go beyond logic.

So he went out, found the huge rock, and began to push it. But the rock did not roll over the cliff. He continued to push for days but was not able to move it an inch. The asuras – the demons, who are not devotees of the Lord Shiva came and told him, "Never join the suras, – angels. If you join them, you will be disappointed. You have been pushing for days yet nothing has happened. Join us and then you will see that you will never be disappointed."

The man was in a real dilemma. Was it true, what the demons — the *asuras* were saying? He pushed and he pushed and sincerely did what the Lord had asked him to do and yet nothing had happened. Maybe, he thought it was better to join the *asuras* — the demons. Not knowing whom to follow, he sat down and for the first time closed his eyes in prayer and chanted, 'Om Namah Shivaya, Om Namah Shivaya'.

First time in his life, he meditated and prayed, "Oh Lord, please help me. I am tempted by the asuras who are asking me to follow them. I have tried my best and put in great effort to push the rock." Once again the divine light appeared in front of him and asked, "What is your disappointment?" "Oh, Lord! I did not deserve your blessings and am fortunate to have got it. You made a request and I have sincerely followed your instructions. I have tried my best to push the rock; not even an inch has it moved. I am so disappointed, so frustrated and have become so despondent." Lord Shiva who was in the form of a light told the Bhakta — devotee, "Why should you feel disappointed? I only told you to push the rock. I did not tell you to push the rock down to the other side of the cliff."

The Lord had asked him to push the rock and this man had interpreted it to mean push the rock down to the other side.

The man asked, "What is the purpose of pushing it?"
Lord Shiva said, "When you pushed the rock, see what
has happened to you. Look at your biceps, look at your
triceps, look at your shoulders, look at your heart, look
at your chest; how healthy, strong and masculine your
body has become. Hasn't your action produced results?
All that pushing has produced such wonderful results."

Please digest the story. Problems come not to trouble
us, but to give us certain strengths that we do not know
we have. We should have *shraddha* – trust that these
problems are here to make us better, and not bitter in
life. Without any *apeksha*, without any expectation you
should do your dharma. Go on doing what is right,
whether the results come or not. You may hit a huge rock
a hundred times with a hammer and when it doesn't
break, you feel that you have wasted all that effort. Just
then a pretty looking girl comes along and touches the
rock and it breaks. You will feel upset that although you
hit it a hundred times, nothing happened and the woman
merely touched and it broke. But remember that your
effort was not wasted. Every time you hit it, cracks
appeared inside which were not visible externally.

When you practice the path of spirituality, visible results
may not be seen but invisible results would happen very
subtly. When the man pushed the rock, it appeared to
have no result. But his biceps, triceps, chest, shoulder

were developed and toughened. So problems make us stronger in life. It is your expectations that make your life bitter. Remember, life makes us stronger, our expectations makes us bitter.

Have you seen how some people get very upset if there is just one grey hair on their head? They come and ask me if there is any mantra for the grey hair to go. When I don't give them a mantra they say that there are so many gurus who give such a mantra. But I am a person who would rather make people think, that is the problem. But people don't want to think.

One day, a man came up to me and said, "Swamiji, if our guru asks us to jump from the fifteenth floor, we will jump. We believe in our guru so much that without even thinking, we will jump Swamiji. Will your shishyas – students do that?"

I told him that my *shishyas* would never do such a thing. If I tell my *shishyas* to jump from the fifteenth floor, they will say that I should jump first and then if I survive they will jump too. I have taught my *shishyas* to think properly. The general tendency of the people is to follow. I don't want followers. I want people who think and create their path. How to make you think is my job. It is said, "While some of us think, many of us think we think and most of us never think of thinking".

Please understand, religion has become a game of leaders and followers; it should be a game of understanding. In your life if you create your inner harmony, nature will help you to be in harmony. Please believe this. Don't believe the ego, which is filled with expectations. God is not an ego, God is a principle, which the eyes can see, the ears can hear and the nose can smell. And if you can trust the principle because of which the eyes can see, the ears can hear and the nose can smell, then the mind can think. You have to only trust the principle.

"*Sutre manigana eva* — Lord Krishna declares in the Bhagavad Gita. I am like a thread which goes through the beads, I am the principle".

In the *Ishavasya* Upanishad you can find these words of the Lord: "*Ishāvasyam idhagum sarvam yat kincha jagatyām jagat*". The Lord says, "I pervade in and through everywhere". The Lord — Isha is everywhere — *vasyam idugm sarvam.*

"Where is Lord Shiva? I don't find HIM everywhere" may be your reaction. As a principle HE exists in your eyes, in your nose, in your lips, when your heart throbs, when your heart stops throbbing, when your liver functions and when your liver stops functioning; because that principle is *srishti sthiti laya.*

The principle, by which creation took place, the principle by which creation is sustained, the principle by which even the creation is destroyed – *laya*, that principle is the Lord, it is Lord Shiva – *"Ishāvasyam idhagum sarvam yat kincha jagatyām jagat"*.

You should learn how to trust this principle. So keep yourself in harmony and nature is going to be in harmony with you. To keep yourself in harmony, you have to do the necessary actions, the right actions, the right karmas, and put in the right effort. Therefore, Lord Shiva says *Udyamo*, the effort *Bhairavaha*, that you put in is Lord Shiva.

Please repeat the sutra after me, *Udyamo Bhairavaha*. It means the effort that you put in the right track that *udyamo*, that effort is indeed *bhairavaha*. If you have made the wrong effort, then the theory of karma is going to work. Fire can give you warmth; fire can also burn you. Don't blame the fire. Your karma can bless you and your karma can destroy you, don't blame the karma.

When we encounter problems in life, remember that problems can happen for two reasons. We attract problems. If you are miserable you attract miserable people; and then somebody else's misery and your misery will do *jugalbandi* and become more miserable.

There are a lot of marriages in which both husband and wife are miserable, being miserable they get married to another miserable person and both these miserable people will do jugalbandi. It is like the man who jumped into the river to commit suicide.

The person who saw him jumping to commit suicide also jumped in to save the other person. Then he realised that he does not know swimming. Both do not know swimming and both drowned each other in their act of saving one another. That is what happens all around. This lady is miserable, that man is miserable and the two miserable people get married. They double their misery with both doing jugalbandi. If you don't know how to play the flute, and your friend does not know how to play the tabla and you do jugalbandi with the flute and the tabla, what kind of music will you create?

So your problems can be of two types. One is you attract misery and so you attract problems in life unnecessarily. You are unhappy and so you smoke. Smoking is not a solution. You may say, "No, I am bored Swamiji. So I smoke." But why did you pick up that smoking habit first? Living in a hot climate as you do, why do you smoke and then come to my workshop to learn how to stop smoking. Maybe you are miserable you attract misery.

The second type of problem can be a problem of difficulties in life. It is because of certain karmas that are fructifying, karmas that you have done before. You have to understand that it is the karma which is fructifying. Any new karma you do will not allow the old karma to cause an impact. If you are a diabetic not by abusing yourself, but because you are genetically prone to diabetes, you may have diabetes because of your DNA or you may say your karma has made you diabetic. But do you say that since you are genetically prone to diabetes you don't do anything about it? No – you exercise, you do yoga, you do pranayama, you do different things; they may or may not cure you of your diabetes but will at least impact your DNA, your genes and will have a positive influence.

Let me give another example for you to understand.

One may be abusing his digestive system by eating five masala dosas early in the morning, four potato vadas at mid morning, two cheese burgers at lunch and so on. He eats all this that he becomes diabetic. You cannot say it is his problem, for it is an abuse of karma. So one can become diabetic because of an abuse of karma, or one can become diabetic because of his DNA. Whatever the cause, good acts like exercise and diet can reduce the diabetes. I am giving this example for you to understand, for in the same way, your problem can be that you live an unintelligent life, and you don't do your homework of studying properly. But when you get married you have to do your homework and learn how to handle marriage. When you have children you do your homework and learn how to bring up children. If you don't do any homework, you mess up your life. That is one kind of problem.

The second is when you do all your homework, you do everything that you can, but you get a wrong partner in life, that is karma.

Therefore your problems can crop up because of your karma, or because of unintelligent living.

The Shiva Purana has yet another beautiful story. Along with the Shiva Sutra, I have also talked about Shiva Purana and the symbol of Lord Shiva. The Shiva Sutra is not in the Shiva Purana, which contains only stories. The Sutras are for much more intelligent people and the ritual of Shiva is a different symbol. Please understand the map here. I am clubbing all three together for easy understanding.

One day, Parvathi saw a poor Lord Shiva's devotee and felt sorry for him. She tried to coax Lord Shiva to help him. "Look at that man, how much he is suffering, have compassion for him, he is your devotee." Lord Shiva told her that even if he helped the devotee, he would not be able to receive the help. Generally, ladies find it difficult to understand such a statement. Parvathi too felt the same and said, "Why? How can that be?" "Alright, you just see what turns out," said Lord Shiva.

The poor man, the Lord Shiva's devotee was walking. It is said that Lord Shiva took a invisible form and went there with a packet full of gold and diamonds. The invisible Shiva dropped the packet in the devotee's path, as he was walking. The poor man saw the packet, opened it and found it to be full of gold and diamonds. He was in deep difficulty. He looked here and there, and saw a bullock cart passing by. He took the packet, ran up to the man seated on the bullock cart and asked him if it were his packet. That man said that it was indeed his packet. He took it and went away.

Then Parvathi realised that if a person does not have the karma to receive, even if somebody gives him something he will not receive it.

If you and I don't have karma, then even if Krishna comes here, or Shiva, Buddha, or Jesus comes here, we will not be able to receive them, for we don't have the karma.

Therefore during the time of Lord Krishna, Dritha-
rashtra could not receive him, nor could Duryodhana.
Just imagine what would have happened if you and I had
been alive at the time of Lord Krishna. Would we have
followed everything? We may think so because Lord
Krishna is not here now. Once he is there, maybe we will
take Him for granted.

Therefore in the Shiva Purana we read of this wonder,
that if you don't have the karma, you would not be able
to receive blessings even if they come to you. So what
should we do then? We should do the right karma
everyday.

Do what Lord Shiva calls *Prayaschita Karma* – '*Yani
kaanicha papani janmani kritanicha kshamaswa kshamswa
kshamaswa.*' What sin that I have done... *Yani kaanicha
papani*, in what *janma*, birth, I have done it I do not
know... *janmani kritanicha kshamaswa*. I ask for forgiveness
as the first step, then I do the good act as a second step;
this is called *prayaschitta karma*.

Therefore understand that our difficulties can be created
in this birth or it can be the result of previous karma
but life is a combination of both. Whatever it is, keep
your self in harmony and do the right action. When you
do the right action, you will find that your whole
perspective will become different.

Drop Inner Poisoning

What is the right action? There are two beautiful sutras in the Shiva Sutra – *Chittam mantraha* and *Visham thyajet*.

Chittam mantraha dwells on the right karma, which is, to lead chittam – the mind, into a mantra.

During one of my workshops in Delhi, I danced with my students for about an hour. One of the participants who saw me dance non-stop felt that I might have taken ganja or drug. He wondered how it was possible for some one to dance at this age for an hour or more. He felt that I must definitely be taking some drugs. My student defended me by asking him to look at my eyes. But he was of the opinion that Swamijis in Delhi take drugs; and was quite disappointed that I did not. Even when I drink buttermilk, they think otherwise.

People always doubt.

What I do in communication is a pre-emptive strike or else one goes on doubting; it is not part of Shiva sutra. If you have such doubts you will not listen to me with rapt attention.

In communication theory this is called a pre-emptive strike. In the Bhagvad Gita Lord Krishna says, "*Samshayaatma vinashayti*" – which means a person who doubts would perish.

Coming back to Shiva Sutra, *chittam mantraha* – your mind should become a mantra. And how does the mind become a mantra? First *Visham thyajet* – avoid poisonous food; poisonous food for the body, poisonous food for the mind, poisonous food for the intellect, poisonous food for the emotion, poisonous food for the soul – all should be avoided, *visham thyajet*.

What is mantra? The meaning of the word mantra is '*mananat trayate iti mantra*'; *manana* means if you reflect, *trayate* means it protects you. *Om Namah Shivaya, Om Namah Shivaya*, it is not only *uchcharana* – utterances, but also *manana* – reflection. What is *namaha*? What is Shivaya? If you liberate – *trayate*, it protects you.

There are two types of impact in a Mantra. The mantra itself is a vibration. In homoeopathy the medicines sulphur, natrum sulph and nux vomica are all nothing but vibrations. You can take the snake poison Lachesis in a small dose; its potencies enter into vibration working as medicine. A part of a certain flower is also taken and put into a machine that extracts its potency, and transforms it into pure vibration. And this vibration, if given in the right dosage, works wonders.

Homeopathy is a science which Hanemann discovered and it works really well if it is administered rightly.

Our Rishis and our yogis discovered the impact of vibration long before *sadashiva samarambham* – since the time of creation. Mantra also creates vibration.

Vibrations are of two types, it can be a negative vibration or a positive one. Our Rishis discovered in those ancient times that vibrations can be both negative and positive.

It is stated that seventy percent of the heart attacks occur due to stress. Stress is due to our problematic life style and problematic working style. If 50% of heart attacks are due to genetic problems, 50% of the heart attacks can be even due to atmospheric factors. Due to external atmosphere and internal atmosphere the stress level goes up. When one is highly stressed out, the adrenaline starts pumping faster; adrenaline prepares you for a flight or fight situation... which in turn makes you get worked up over small things. Your adrenaline is your emergency gland that pumps adrenal and it is going to affect the heart; thus apart from genetic causes, this too can cause heart attack – so one's working style has to be different.

What is stress? Again, it is a vibration. But it is a negative vibration.

If there is a negative, there has to be positive. If there is white, there must be black. If there is darkness there must be light. If there is night there must be day. So if there are negative vibrations there must be positive vibrations. Our yogis have done a lot of research in positive vibrations and the outcome of the research is the *tantra, yantra* and *mantras*. They have also found that different *raags,* notes like the bhairav raag, or the *hamsadhvani* have different impacts; *Revathi* has a different impact, *Malkauns* has another impact, Raag *Durg* has some other impact. Therefore raagas have different impacts.

Even exercises have varied impacts. When one does Tai-Chi exercise the impact is different from that of aerobics.

When you practice martial arts, it impacts you differently from yoga. When you walk on a treadmill, it is a different impact from walking in open air. So too every vibration has different impacts.

To produce positive vibrations, the Rishis have created certain combinations of words which are the mantras and these mantras create certain vibrations.

You find in Vedic mantras every syllable has a certain intonation; the voice goes up for one syllable and comes down for another syllable; another syllable has to go *swarita*. When you learn the Vedic chants every syllable has to go up and down so arithmetically, that it creates a tremendous vibration.

The famous Gayathri Mantra has to be chanted as follows.

Om Bhur Buva Suvaha – here the 'va' has to go down

Om Bhur Buva swaha – this 'va' has to go up

Om tatsa – the 'sa' has to be down, up

Om tatsa vi – 'vi' has to go down

Om tatsa viturvarenyam – 'ye' is swarita; 'nyam' has to go down. *'Bhargo'* – 'go' has to go up

Devasya 'de' has to be down; *yasya* – 'ya' has to go up

Dheemahi – no combination there

Dhiyo – 'yo' has to go down

Yo na – 'yo' no combination; na has to go up

Prachod ayat – 'cho' has to go down.

When you chant this way, the intonation creates certain vibrations.

This is how the Gayathri Mantra has to be chanted. And when you chant the mantra in this manner, *"manana trayate iti mantraha"*. When you chant the mantra, it protects you with its vibration and with its meaning.

What is the meaning?

Right now we are talking on Lord Shiva. Om Namah Shivaya. It is not in the Shiva sutra. This is a mantra on Lord Shiva. Om Namah Shivaya. When you say Om Namah Shivaya, Om means fullness. The upanishad

called Mandukya Upanishad elaborates on this. Let me
not go into it.

Om means fullness. Life is full — *poornamadaha
poornamidam poornath poornamudachchate.* Om means full.
Now how can you say life is full?

I will say a little and confuse you further. Om is full,
life is full. This moment is full. This moment is complete. It is Om. But we don't experience completeness.
We don't experience completeness, because a thought
comes into our mind and says, one year ago my bank
balance was different and in the future it may become
worse; thus I become incomplete, not because of the moment but because of thought. This moment is complete.
But my thoughts take me back two years and I compare.
Two years ago I was like this, yesterday I was like this;
my thought goes back to yesterday and my thought goes
to the future and therefore thought creates incompleteness. By going to the past and going to the future, my
thoughts make me experience incompleteness. Not that
I am incomplete, it is the thought that is incomplete.

Who is the sucker? It is the thought.

Mantra – Creating
Mystical Fullness

The great Pathanjali puts it beautifully, *chitta vritti nirodhaha* is yoga. Eliminate such thoughts, he says. You may ask, "Swamiji, if I should not have thought, if I should not compare, how is it possible for me to progress Swamiji?"

In Vedanta we say thoughts are of two types. One is enlightened thought and the other is unenlightened thought. This moment is complete. When thought compares the past and the future and makes it incomplete, what type of comparison are you making? It is an unenlightened thought. When it compares with the past, it whips itself, when it compares with the future, it whips itself too. This whipping thought of comparison is called *agnyana vritti.*

In Vedanta *agnyana vritti* is ignorant thought. Now what is called as *gnana vritti,* is also called *brahmakara vritti* – *vritti* means thought. This moment is complete but I still compare it with yesterday, I still compare it with the future, but when I compare it with yesterday and compare it with the future, I don't whip myself, I only compare for the joy of comparing and then say, "Aha, yesterday was a unique experience, today is a unique experience, tomorrow it can be a unique experience." I compare and in the process of comparison I don't belittle myself, I don't whip myself, I don't smash myself, I don't victimise myself. I don't ravage myself – such a thought, such a comparison is *brahmakara vritti. Brahma* means fullness, *akara* means form, and *vritti* means thought.

So if you have an enlightened thought, no problem. If you have an unenlightened thought then it is a problem. Thus, life is not the problem, it is the thought which is the problem. In fact thought is not the problem; it is the unenlightened thought which is a problem.

So when Pathanjali says *chitta vritti nirodhaha,* what type of thought is he talking of? Unenlightened thought. Since unenlightened thought gives you negative vibrations, therefore *chittam mantraha*. Let your *chittam*, your mind, be a mantra; mantra means positive vibration.

Thought is a vibration. But with negative vibrations you feel miserable. Positive vibrations make you feel full. So when you say Om, it means fullness.

Therefore, the beautiful mantra *poorna madaha poornamidam*... means that is full, this is full and everything is full. And Om means fullness.

So, Om Namah Shivaya. Look at the word Namaha – Na Ma, put Ma before Na; what does it become? It becomes *Manaha* – mind. At present, we have *manaha*; what type of *manaha*? It is negative *manaha*. Hence, you have Bhakti gnana, which says that manaha should become namaha. The ma-na should do upside down. Na goes before ma, ma goes after na, and it becomes Namaha, meaning surrender. Therefore, chant Om Namaha Shivaya. And we have already learnt about Shivaya.

If you can understand in Sanskrit *sham mangalam karoti iti shivaha*, it is enough; it will take you to ecstasy. If you don't know the Sanskrit word Shiva symbolically, I have already explained to you earlier that the tiger represents six qualities. Quickly, what are those six qualities? Vision, power, commitment, speed, strategy and skill.

When you have imbibed the quality of Shiva, you would acquire all the six qualities.

What does trishula mean? *Satvaguna, rajo guna, tamoguna*, meaning you should be a master of your qualities; the qualities should not be your master. I have explained to you elaborately earlier what *sattva* means, what *rajas* means and what *tamas* means. *Rajas* is activity. Are you doing activity or action? We are lost in activity; activity means we are escaping from the self. Most of our activities are an escape from oneself. Action is not an escape from oneself. Action is a consciously done act.

We are lost in activity. Most people, when they get bored, watch either TV show or go for a movie or go to a kitty party.... What do they do at the kitty party? Simply gossip. There is no substance in their talk, because they want to escape from themselves and that is activity. And where do these activities come from? From the fear and greed.

Don't we have to be very active, Swamiji?

Active means action not activity. Rajas is activity. You have to be in action and action has no fear or greed, but your activity is filled with fear and greed.

The *trishula* as I was saying represents sattva, rajas, and tamas. The *trishula* has the *damaru* hanging around it, we have already learnt the meaning of *damaru; I wun wul ruk ye won aih auch...* means the intuition by which Panini discovered the sutras and Pathanjali interpreted the same. All these represent the mystical sounds that are created right here. You need a receptor to receive the mystical sounds and that is the power of intuition.

What else does Lord Shiva hold? Lord Shiva has a *Kamandalu*. What else? A Japa Mala. That Japa mala means *chittam mantraha*, and that is where I am trying to unfold the connection. In one hand Shiva carries a kamandalu and a japa mala. The moment you see a japamala in anybody's hand it means *chittam mantraha*, because a mantra is chanted in five stages.

Listen carefully. You take the Japamala, you chant *Om Namah Shivaya* and turn the bead; again *Om Namah Shivaya* and then turn a bead; yet again, *Om Namah Shivaya*, turn a bead. But in reality, this is what happens: *Om Namah Shivaya*, turn a bead, *Om Namah Shivaya* turn a bead, what happens next? The thought that Shivaswamy from Sri Lanka did not return the money – from Shivaswamy you go to Sri Lanka, from Sri Lanka you go to the drug movement, from drug movement to Rajiv Gandhi's killing, their link with terrorists and it goes on through out the world and with what did you start off? *Om Namah Shivaya*.

If you see the mind, it connects from somewhere to somewhere else. When you say using the japamala *Om Namah Shivaya* and turn a bead, *Om Namah Shivaya* and turn a bead, then Shivaswamy... what happens is that you stop turning the beads. When you stop, through the sensing of the beads, the mind is reminded that something has gone wrong. So the Japamala is a very good aid. Don't chant *Om Namah Shivaya* hundred and eight times to make Lord Shiva's kundalini go up. It is not to please Lord Shiva that you turn hundred and eight beads.

When you chant *Om Namah Shivaya,* the mind wanders like a monkey, somebody even said like a drunken monkey. Not only a drunken monkey, but one bitten by a scorpion. If there is some instrument to check how your mind works and some parameter for your wife to know what is in your mind or for the husband to know what is in his wife's mind, the husband and wife can never stay together, I vouch you. It is good that God in His infinite wisdom has not shown us what is in our mind. That is why the mind is like a drunken monkey that is bitten by a scorpion.

I am talking about Shiva sutra and you are wondering if Swamiji is married? What connection? I already feel someone in the crowd thinking it. I have intuitive powers. Another person wonders, "Before becoming a

Swamiji, did he have an affair? He looks so smart that he surely must have had one. Poor girl, why did she leave him?" I am talking about *Om Namah Shivaya* and the mind goes from somewhere to somewhere to somewhere else like a drunk monkey bitten by a scorpion. So the mind goes here and there, and therefore you take the aid of the japamala; *Om Namah Shivaya*, turn a bead, *Om Namah Shivaya* turn a bead, when the mind wanders, it stops turning. This is an indication given to your mind, 'Hey, come back to *Om Namah Shivaya.*' But again, the mind goes somewhere else. So you train with the help of the japamala to bring the mind to the present and not just to count hundred and eight beads.

So the first stage is *Om Namah Shivaya*, the second stage is when you drop the japamala. The japamala is in the hands of Lord Shiva – *chittam mantraha*; there are four to five stages to chanting mantras; one is japamala, second is, when use of japamala is stopped. Once you develop a little mastery of your mind, you should not use the japamala. You should go beyond it.

Simply say *Om Namah Shivaya, Om Namah Shivaya*; when you do that you should feel that the Om is complete. Namaha actually means 'nothing in the mind'. When you perform a havan – a ritual of sacred fire, actually you are asked to do na mama and pour the ghee; na mama and pour the ghee, na mama and pour the ghee. Na mama means not mine, not mine, not mine. Na mama, na mama, na mama, na maha, na maha — that is the etymological origin of the word namaha. Na mama means namaha, nothing is mine, and therefore namaha means humility. Thus, we say Om Namaha Shivaya.

If you have really been brought up with *samskara* — with true Indian culture (unfortunately it has now become diluted), then you realise that there are five stages of japa. The first stage is with japamala, the second stage is with the meaning *Om Namah Shivaya, Om Namah Shivaya*. Om is complete right now, next you have to use it and feel it — you have to feel that this moment is complete. In fact it cleanses your brain and that is why it has become brainwashing. We are brainwashed, so we have to cleanse our brain. We are told we are incomplete, we are told that without diamond earrings we are incomplete, without a house we are incomplete; we have been hypnotised, so we have to de-hypnotise ourselves in order to be complete.

So, during the second stage of japamala when you chant *Om Namah Shivaya, Om Namah Shivaya*, feel the vibration, feel the *artha*, feel the meaning, live that meaning. You have to live that *Om Namah Shivaya*, you have to live, as Kalidasa says in Raghuvamsha, "*Vak kartha iva sampruktau vak karta pratipattaye jagatah pitarau vande parvathi parameshwarau*" — between *vak* and *artha* — the word and the meaning, there is *sampruktau* – it is united. It is united like Parvathi and Parameshwara. So the word and meaning should be united – that is why if your name is Shanti, you have to be Shanti – peace. If I am Swami Sukhabodhananda and my name means *sukhena bhodhayati*, one who very easily teaches, *Asau Anandaha* – and blissfully. Now, I should be true to the name. If your name is Vidyasagar – you have to be one with vidya. So Kalidas says *vak arthayiva sampruktauv* – it should be united. If your name is Smitha – smile, learn to smile.

Once, on a Lufthansa Airlines flight, something went wrong. The pilot announced, "Sorry, we have to land on the sea. Don't panic. We have the facility to land on the sea". The passengers were scared. The Airhostess said again with a wide smile, "Don't panic, we have the facility to land on the sea; all those who know swimming come to the left side of the plane and all those who do not know swimming come to the right side of the plane." Some came to the left and some went to the right. Again she said, "Thank you for following my instructions. All those people who know swimming please jump and swim to the shore." Again with a smile, "The distance is only fifty miles. All those people who do not know swimming…" again with a smile, "… thank you for flying with Lufthansa." What type of thank you is this? Don't get into such courtesies.

Your smile does not mean simply elongating your lips like an airhostess smile. No. Let your smile be gentle, genuine. When you chant Om, just feel it. Even if it is not happening to you, feel, it is not happening, feel. Even if you don't get the feeling, feel, only then the feeling centre in you will open up.

That is why it is always good to learn some art. "*Sangeeta sahitya kala rahitaha pashu samanaha*," is a saying in Sanskrit. If you don't know *sangeet*a – music, if you don't know *sahitya* – literature or *kala* – any art, then you are *pashu samanaha* – equal to an animal. When you know a *kala*, an art then you know how much of effort you have to put in. Please understand this very clearly – Om means feel the fullness. Even though you don't feel it, try to feel it. *Namaha* means nothing is really mine. Tell me what is mine? Even this moustache is not mine, without my effort it will drop. My teeth will also fall out, for nothing is mine. When nothing is mine how can you say that your wife is yours? Then who is she, Swamiji? Let God answer that. You are only a trustee, nothing is yours.

Really, nothing is mine.

The first stage is japamala. The second is japa where only the mantra is chanted with feeling. Now, we come to the third stage in japa – Om namahshivaya, Om namahshivaya, Om namahshivaya – feel the silence between two mantras, feel the silence. Please look at my hands; there is gap between two fingers. This is the mantra, there is the silence. Between two mantras there is silence. So the third stage of japa is to feel the silence.

The observer of silence becomes silence. So, mantra and silence, mantra and silence. In the Bhagavad, there is a reference to Raasleela. In Raasleela, all the Gopis dance and Lord Krishna is in the centre and the devotees are circled on the periphery. When we see there are the Gopis and there is Lord Krishna. How many Lord Krishnas are there? Only one Lord Krishna. But that one Lord Krishna is placed in the centre. The circle is made of Gopis; Gopis mean thoughts. When it is said that Lord Krishna is married to 16,000 gopis, it does not mean that he has physically married 16,000 gopis. Gopis are thoughts. Therefore, there are 16,000 thoughts and at the centre of these thoughts is Lord Krishna and you are a *sakshi* – a witness. If you are a witness and have observed that the Gopis are thoughts, then who is there between two Gopis? Between two gopis is Lord Krishna and again, between the next two gopis is Lord Krishna and that is why we say Gopi-Krishna, Gopi-Krishna, Gopi-Krishna... And what is Lord Krishna? Silence. Between two thoughts there is silence.

Similarly, Om Namahshivaya, silence, Om Namahshivaya, silence. The first stage is with Japamala, the
second stage is to feel the mantra, the third stage is to
chant the mantra, and observe the silence. In the fourth
stage chant the mantra, give a big pause and just be with
the silence. *Chidambaram Chidakashaha*, be more in the
silence, less in the mantra. Silence is the greatest of all
vibrations.

Classical music emerged from silence. No music can ever
exist without the backdrop of silence. Have you thought
over the fact that if there is no silence, music can never
be created? It is only against the contrast of silence that
music is created. There has to be a platform for the
sound to emerge. If everything is sound, the very sound
itself is a catastrophe.

Therefore, mantra is silence. When you are chanting the
mantra, get into the fourth stage and then don't chant.
Keep the silence for a long time. Then you will know
how to get into silence.

In the fifth stage don't even chant the mantra. Only
silence. In the Shaivite tradition this is called
Chidambaram. It is also called *Chidakashaha*.

There is a place called Chidambaram in Tamil Nadu.

There, they perform *arathi* to an empty space, which is silence. And they say *chidambara rahasyam* – *rahasyam* means secret. What do you see if you can keep the mind empty? Next to empty space, there is a *murthy* – idol of Nataraja who is dancing in ecstasy. This means when you are in silence, you start dancing in ecstasy.

It would also be appropriate to know the significance of Rudraksha Mala. Rudraksha Mala has 108 beads which in turn represents 108 upanishads. One should garland one's life with the vision and teachings of enlightened masters representing Rudraksha Mala. Ordinarily, people garland their life with wordly means but a spiritual aspirant takes recourse to enlightened masters. This should be constantly remembered since forgetfulness, more often is our failure. Rudraksha Mala has certain positive energy which in turn stimulates spiritual energy in us.

This constant touch should be our spiritual conection and part of "self remembering".

This is the symbolic meaning of Rudraksha Mala. This understanding should be spiritual ornamentation as compared to wordly ornamentation.

Thus, the five stages of japa. Om Nama Shivaya – Na

maha — nothing is mine, Shivaya — Lord Shiva represents all the qualities of tiger. The trishula, the Japa with its five stages. And Lord Shiva also has *kamandalu* — a pot of water. What does the *kamandalu* represent? It represents simplicity. So lead a simple life.

15

Simplicity – True
Inner Richness

What is meant by simple life? Oh! Simple life – does it mean wearing only underwear? *"Kaupina vanthaha khalu bhagyavanthaha"* – that is not simple. A lot of people misunderstood spirituality and therefore, made spirituality impractical. Simplicity means not something physical but something psychological.

I will give you the psychological meaning – you should be simple, innocent like a child. Please understand that when you are innocent like a child, you are not complicated. When you are complicated you maneuver, manipulate and settle scores. In the corporate world, for instance, each one is busy finding fault with others. When I conduct corporate programmes, I do the following process – I divide the group into two sections and to one section I give balloons, and to the other section I give needles.

The group with the needles goes and punctures every balloon in the other group. All the balloons burst. I ask them, "Why did you do that?" They ask me, "Then what was the purpose?" I have given them the balloon to put up and pin it. I said, "This is exactly what you are doing in the corporate world. You see somebody's success and you puncture it. You are all busy poking at each other." In every organisation you find that somebody does similar act. One man says, "I have done the work and they have taken credit." The other person says "I have done this." Everyone is busy with such complications. Then you maintain a score, and afterwards you settle scores. But when you practice simplicity, you don't get into all this. Thus, *Kamandalu* represents simplicity – an innocent way of looking at life.

See the object as though you are seeing it for the first time. I am giving you the translation for the sloka which is complicated. To practice simplicity, you have to follow two important disciplines. To put it in philosophical terms, one discipline of simplicity has to be in the present. To be in the present is very simple. Where does life show up? In the present, past or future? The present.

Where do we live? In the past and in the future. Very few of us live in the present. Do you know why we cannot live in this moment? Have you observed how, while taking bath, you think of breakfast, while at breakfast, you think of your boss, when you meet the boss, then you think of your wife. When you meet your wife, you think of the boss's wife. Your mind flies like a *kati pathang* – kite, here and there. Why can't you think about your bath when you take a bath? Be in the present; when you go to the toilet, just feel it. You don't have to smell it, just feel it. Let me tell you, it is such a great experience to ease in the toilet. How beautifully the body sewage system cleanses.

We cannot be in this moment from moment to moment, because our mind is riddled with kama, krodha, lobha, moha, mada and matsarya. It is called *shadvikaras* – it is an Upanishadic statement. And the mind is complicated with our desires.

I am giving you this psychodrama only to show that we are very complicated; we are not simple as we think, we are filled with desires. When a man gets married, he thinks, "Aiyo, I should have two wives". But you cannot afford to have two wives.

Please understand that simplicity does not mean wearing a simple dress. I have seen many people who are complicated by being simple. They say, for instance, that they never carry any money, or travel by vehicle. However, behind them is a caravan of vehicles carrying food for these persons while they go on a pada yatra. They do not carry any money but there are many people walking behind who carry money for them. It is my duty to educate you about all this. It is only to impress others that you appear to be simple and get compressed. Simplicity is not what you wear but a simple thing to wear. Really, simplicity can be just in this moment.

When you are looking at a flower, just look at the flower. When you are looking at a light, just look at it. Be complete in the given moment. *Poornamidam*. This moment is going to be complete. And you can be complete, but you are not because kama, krodha, moha, lobha, mada and matsarya are playing havoc. If we can drop all these and just be in the present, I tell you, psychologi-cally, you are very simple.

"Oh, Swamiji, I am in the present but what about my future?"

"If you want to plan for your future, don't worry".

"Ok, this is my future. This is the investment I have to make".

"Plan for it but live in the present, plan for the future".

"What about my past"?

Learn from the past, don't live in the past. We live in the past and worry about the future and we miss the present. This is a very complicated way of living.

One day, a woman asked me, "Swamiji, I have a lot of tension because of my daughter." I asked, "Why?" "It is my daughter. She has asthma, Swamiji, therefore who will marry her?" I asked whether she had brought her. She had. Her daughter was a 4-year old kid, and she was worrying about who would marry her daughter. I told her that there can be another asthma patient who may love her, and these two asthma patients can marry and play *jugalbandi*.

Look, how things are made complicated. After all, who knows, the asthma may go away. And what is so terrible about asthma? It creates a little difficulty while breathing. I find that asthma patients often live longer because of the natural pranayama protecting them.

What is simplicity? Living in the moment. If you have

to plan, plan it but don't live in the future. You have to learn from the past, learn but don't live there. Have you seen how some people keep talking about the past? Parents keep talking about 'my days, my days'. Thus they live in the past.

Simplicity also means to be in harmony with what is. A simple person is one who is at peace with what is. If a grey hair is seen, be in harmony. Why dye it unnecessarily? Have you seen how people dye their hair and develop skin rashes? I have seen young girls with black hair that they have dyed brown. If God has given them brown hair, they make it purple. The first time I saw a Punk, in Australia, I thought he was an alien, for he had black, purple, and yellow hair all sticking up. I was hardly 24 years old when I saw that punk. How unnecessarily we mess up. Why do we color our hair like this and that too with so many shades of color!

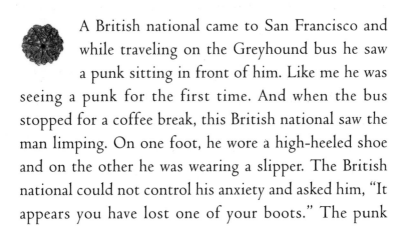 A British national came to San Francisco and while traveling on the Greyhound bus he saw a punk sitting in front of him. Like me he was seeing a punk for the first time. And when the bus stopped for a coffee break, this British national saw the man limping. On one foot, he wore a high-heeled shoe and on the other he was wearing a slipper. The British national could not control his anxiety and asked him, "It appears you have lost one of your boots." The punk

replied, "No, I found one boot and picked it up." People pick up unnecessary things and suffer.

Somebody went to Mullah Nasruddin and asked, "I have a tremendous stomach ache, please help me. I want my stomach ache to go at any cost." Mullah paused for a while, took a big stone and smashed it on his leg. Unable to bear the pain the man screamed loudly and questioned Mullah, "Why did you do that? Mullah said, "Now you will not have stomach ache, you will only have leg pain."

So to get over one problem, you invite another problem. This is called complicated living. Then you take drugs, ecstasy, crack, cocaine and then ask if there is any yoga or pranayam to drop the drug. First tell me why you took drugs. All these things are the opposite of simplicity.

Simplicity first means to be in the moment. And the moment is really complete. It is the thought that is incomplete. Second, simplicity means be in harmony with what is. Once you learn to be in harmony with what is, then you will not create conflict with what is. Complicated people create conflict with what is. Simple people will create harmony with what is.

Om Namah Shivaya.

16

Dropping the Inner Desire

Lord Shiva has a snake around him. The snake represents desire. A snake is dangerous, but the dangerous snake on Lord Shiva's neck is harmless because it has no poison. The snake around Shiva's neck has no poison and hence it represents no desire. It is not *dhooshana* – stark, it is *bhooshana* – Ornamentation or Opulent.

Desire is not a problem; the poison of desire is a problem. What is the poison of desire? "I want to become happy", says one man. We are lost in the "becoming" domain; we are not in the "being" domain. We are always lost in the becoming domain but we are not in the being domain. I am talking for happiness when I am in the

becoming domain. If I talk out of happiness then I am
in the being domain. If I talk for popularity, then I am
in the becoming domain. *Samsara* is in the becoming
domain. Always desire is not the problem, but desire
always wants to become something. Even to become
something is not a problem, but when you feel that only
if you become something will you be happy – this feeling
creates problem. So we postpone happiness by putting
it in the future. The feeling "I want to become" is not
a problem. The belief that "When I become... only then
I will be happy" is a problem.

Happiness is not the result of your desire being fulfilled
and happiness is not the result of your desire not being
fulfilled. That is the great teaching in the Shiva sutra.
Happiness is not the result of your desire being fulfilled
or not being fulfilled. Your desire should come from
happiness. If you are in that vibration frequency, it is
called *chittam mantraha*. What is the mantra? Om Namah
Shivaya. Shiva's snake represents this.

What does the Moon on Lord Shiva's head mean? A calm
mind. Ganga flowing from Lord Shiva's head is the *gnana
nadi* – the river of understanding. If you take a bath in
the Ganges your paapa, your sins are gone. This
symbolically represents that if you take a bath in the river
of understanding – Ganges, then all your sins –
misunderstandings or ignorance would wash away. If you

are an *upasaka*, then every quality of Shiva *avahanam samarpayaami*, would be invoked within you. Therefore, please understand *chittam mantraha*. Your mind should become a mantra; the mantra is Om Namah Shivaya.

If you are an *upasaka*, you are invoking Lord Shiva, if you are not an *upasaka*, and you are an agnani, remember, Om means fullness, namaha means this – Shiva means *mangalam karoti iti shiva*.

Chittam mantraha. The next sutra is *visham thyajet* – visham means poisonous food – *thyajet*, you should give up. This is indeed a beautiful sutra if you can practice it in your life. *Visham thyajet* – give up or drop poisonous food. What is poisonous food? Please understand that there is food for the body, food for the emotion, food for the mind. Just as there is healthy food for the body and poisonous food for the body, there is healthy food for your emotion and poisonous food for the emotion; there is healthy food for your mind, there is poisonous food for the mind. Therefore, if you can learn to drop all that is poisonous then it is *visham thyajet*.

I would like you to practice this. For example, let us take up emotion. Every moment if you have negative emotion, then give it away – thyajet, thyajet, thyajet. If you feel jealous of somebody then say "No" to the feeling – chittam mantraha. If you feel jealous of somebody, please

chant, Om Namah shivaya. Then chaitanya atma —
become more aware. Why are you feeling jealous? Don't
use the mantra to escape. Use the mantra to transform.
Then why are you having jealousy? Look for the clarity
on which I have already unfolded. When you seek clarity
you may realise that jealousy is making you incomplete.
Don't you think jealousy is just a movement of thought?
It is a movement of emotion. What is emotion? Energy
in motion is emotion. Understand that the quality of
your life is the quality of your consistent emotion. If
you have negative emotions, your life will be miserable.

I have given the following example in my book.

A man was begging the Lord to fulfill his
desires. The Lord said, "If I fulfill your desires
you will still be unhappy." The man said, "Oh
Lord, you mind your own business. You only fulfill my
desire. Your job is to fulfill and my job is to receive.
God's nature is to give." So, God said, "I will fulfill
whatever desire you have but on one condition." "What
is the condition?" God said, "Whatever boon you get,
others will get double of the same." He said, "I am not
bothered if others get double. As long as I get what I
want, there is no problem." *Tatastu* - so be it, said the
Lord.

The man chanted Om Namah shivaya and said, "I want

a beautiful bungalow"; immediately a bungalow appeared before him. He felt extremely happy. My God! What a wonderful bungalow! But when he went out, he found that everybody had got two such bungalows. Although he knew that God had said this would happen, he could not digest that fact. Then the man prayed for wonderful interiors for his house. Immediately, it was ready. But when he saw the others' bungalows they were twice as grand. Then he wanted a Mercedes Benz, and immediately a Mercedes Benz appeared in front of his gate. But the others got two Mercedes Benz cars.

Whatever he got, the others got two times more of that. He was very jealous for he thought that he had put in the effort and those rascals were benefiting.... that too doubly. He had performed tapas and whatever God gave him, those rascals too were getting. He told himself, "I will teach those rascals a lesson. They are not even grateful to me." He forgot that the property that the others got were not his to begin with. Once a business-man, always a businessman. He decided to teach them a lesson. So he prayed to the Lord to take away one of his eyes. Immediately he lost one eye.

He went out and saw that everyone had become blind. And then he felt elated that everybody had become blind for he still had one eye. But with his one eye, he had to see everybody suffering because of their blindness. They were blind in both eyes and he could see their suffering. Thus, he became unhappy.

You see how negative emotion will make you erratic.

Therefore, we say *visham thyajet* – drop poisonous food, drop poisonous emotion, drop poison from your mind. If all the poisons can be dropped from your system, and if you can be in this discipline of being non-poisonous, your very being will be *chittam mantraha*. And when your *chittam* is *mantraha*, then *atma nartakaha*, means you will always be dancing out of ecstasy. You will revel in a state of deep ecstasy.

This state of ecstasy is what Lord Shiva is inviting us to experience. Lord Shiva is also called Nataraja. Raja means King, nata means dancer. He is dancing on a demon; the demon represents our poisonous ego. That is why he is dancing so blissfully. Hence, the word Hindu means *heenam nashayati iti* – Hindu. What keeps you low is heenam; destroy what keeps you low – nashayati. What keeps you low is the visham that you feed your body, the visham you feed your emotion and the visham you feed you mind. If you start dropping these poisons, then you will experience a state of *atma nartakaha*. This is the vision of the Hindu.

17

Creating the Spiritual Armor

I was dwelling on this mantra from Shiva Sutra called *Chittam mantraha*. Chittam means your mind should become a mantra. What is mantra? *Manana trayate iti mantraha*; manana means not only *uchcharana* — utterances, not only should you chant but also *mananath*, you should chant with understanding, *trayate* means you are protected.

In the Bhagavad Gita Lord Krishna unfolds, "Oh Arjuna, if you practice my teaching *swalpam api asya dharmasya trāyate mahato bhayāt* — even if you practice a little you are protected tremendously.

How can one be protected? When you are chanting the

mantra, the vibrations of the mantra create a protective shield around you, and when you chant with meaning, this too creates a protective shield around you. In the Indian culture this protective shield is called *Satsanga Kavacha* — *kavacha* means armor. *Satsanga* means with good association — a protective armor would be created around you.

In Hindu tradition there is a mention of *Anganyasa* and *Karanyasa*. I teach this in my E-LAB workshop. I teach everybody to keep their hands at their *Shikha* or back side of head and utter a mantra, and keep their hands on their arms and then utter a mantra. This is called Anganyasa. Then you do the mudra, which is called Karanyasa. When you chant the mantra and perform Anganyasa and Karanyasa properly, the positive affirmations get into your system.

For example, keep your hands at the heart-centre and the mantra is, "I will have unconditional devotion towards the Lord". Keep your hand at the top of your head and chant "I will always be blissful in life." Keep your hand a little behind the Shikha and then chant "I am always a student of life", keep your hands around your arms and say, "I will always learn to give". "If I serve this universe, the universe will serve me". This is called Anganyasa. I have told it in English although it is in Sanskrit.

When you do this you are always blissful in life, when you go on saying this, it will create a kavacha – armor around you. If you don't create armor around you, then when somebody talks to you negatively, when somebody is jealous of you, it will hit you and pierce through you. Generally what we have is a *samsara kavacha*. We have an armour of *samsara* and thus, when somebody utters something unpleasant, somebody just cracks a joke about us, we get shattered.

I have seen in my workshops that when I crack jokes some people get very hurt. Arrey, I did not mean to hurt them, but they get hurt. But they should understand that because *samsara kavacha* is their aura field, their energy field is very poor and depleted.

Lord Shiva tells Parvati a beautiful sutra, "*Shakthi sandhane shareera utpattihi*". If you are united to my teachings – *shakthi sandhane, shareera* means a new energy, *utpattihi* – a new body gets created. It becomes a spiritual body. And when a spiritual body is created, not a physical body, it is like protective armour. Now if somebody utters something unpleasant to you, it will not pierce through you; like the bullet-proof car, which gets impacted but protects the person within, the spiritual body that is created will protect you.

You have to question what armour are you wearing? A

spiritual person creates a new body, which creates armour around. If you are not a spiritual person, you have a *samsara vastra* around you, a *samsara vastra* which will allow even small things to hurt you, small things to upset you. Lord Krishna says in the Bhagavad Gita, for a wise person, *"Dukkeshu anudvignamanāh sukheshu vigatasprhah"*. Dukkeshu – in the most unpleasant situation, *anudvignamanāh* – you are unruffled; *sukheshu* – even in the pleasant situation or if somebody praises you, *vigatasprhah* – you are not ruffled by people's praise. Unfortunately some people get so excited when praised, that they get a heart attack!

 Have you seen during cricket matches how some people get very excited and then die of it? One man had a heart attack and he was in the hospital. The reason was that he had many daughters and none of them were married. So everyday, on her way home the wife would buy lottery tickets to win money for daughter's marriage. As luck would have it, one day she won the lottery of Rs. 40 lakh. She rushed to the hospital to tell her husband that she had won Rs. 40 lakhs and so all their daughters could get married easily.

As she rushed to the hospital, she met the doctor. The doctor asked the reason for her happiness. She mentioned about winning of the lottery. The doctor warned her not to tell the husband immediately as he may get another heart attack out of sheer happiness. She asked him what she should do. If she didn't tell him, worrying about the daughters could cause another heart attack. The doctor who was a psychiatrist had also learnt homeopathy. He suggested that the husband be given homeopathic doses of joy, which his heart can bear.

So they went in, and the psychiatrist begins to talk to the husband, Mr. Ramaswamy.

"If you win Rs. 1 lakh in a lottery what will you do?"

"First, I will get my 35 year old daughter married, and give her lots of gifts".

"If you win Rs. 2 lakhs what will you do?"

"I will get my second daughter married.

What will you do if you win Rs. 3 Lakhs?"

This continued for some time.

Finally, the psychiatrist asked the patient, "If you get Rs. 40 lakhs what will you do?" The patient wondered why this Doctor was continually raising the amount; he felt that the doctors are dangerous creed, and so he said, "If I get Rs. 40 lakhs, I will give you Rs. 10 lakhs, Doctor."

The psychiatrist got a heart attack and died. He had not expected it! Lord Krishna said, '*Dukkeshu anudvignamanāh sukheshu vigatasprhah*' – even in sukha, one is unruffled. Please understand that if you are really a Shiva bhakta and if you practice whatever has been taught to you, a *Gnana kavacha* – armor of understanding would be created around you.

That is why while doing *Sandhya vandana* – Vedic prayer, one should do *Anganyasa and Karanyasa*, as a kavacha would be created around him. This kavacha – armor, as Lord Shiva says, is the *shareera utpatihi*. When you are doing your exercises there is an energy field around you, and if you observe people doing exercise, you find that their aura is different. People who eat pani puri everyday for breakfast and lunch have a different body structure. Similarly, if you practice spirituality, your eyes will be lustrous with an effulgent aura around you. The sign of spirituality is not what you are saying; it is not even what you are doing, it is who you are. It is your presence.

There is a Hassidic expression, which says 'Who you are speaks so loudly I cannot hear what you are saying'. Words have a secondary presence there.

That is what Lord Shiva means when He says, *chittam mantraha*. Let your mind become a mantra. Mantra means positive vibration, You will have an aura around you, a nirvana kavacha around you. You will have a gnana kavacha called a satsanga kavacha.

What happens when you chant the mantra?

First you understand the mind,

Second you transform the mind, and

Third you transcend the mind.

The quintessence of yoga is in three sentences. First you have to understand the mind. A lot of people don't know the mind.

In my workshop if I ask what is mind, they only say 'Mind your own business Swamiji'. A lot of people don't know what mind is. A lot of people don't realise that more than the events of life, it is the mental states that disturb us. We all think that the situation disturbs us, but no, it is only our mental state that disturbs us. A spiritual person is not focused on the events of life. A spiritual person can understand his mental state. He works on the internal states of the mind. So, first understand the mind.

Saint Kabir said, *"Manke haar haar hai manke jeet jeet"*. The second stage is when you transform the mind from

negative mind to positive mind. Any state comes from
either a negative state or a positive state. You have to
transform your mind and work on it every time.

You may get fired from your job, but if you are a Shiva
bhakta — devotee, a real devotee, you will tell yourself
"Hey, all difficulties are a divine surgery; there must be
a purpose for this difficulty. Let it make me better and
not bitter." A devotee always feels that worrying is insul-
ting God's wisdom and he will never worry. Honestly,
if you are a devotee you will never worry. You will act,
you will be concerned, but you will not be worried. There
is a difference between concern and being worried.

Therefore, to understand the mind, transform the mind,
and transcend the mind is an important part of
spirituality. One must go beyond the mind.

18

Worry is like a Rocking Chair

I have explained to you about mantra-silence, mantra-silence, and mantra-silence. Try to see the silence, the silence that is beyond the mind. In our state of deep sleep, God has given us the experience of existing without the mind. In sleep you don't have a mind – "*aham kimapina jaanami sukena maya nidra anubhuyate*", as Adi Shankracharya said.

Aham kimapina jaanami – I don't know anything, but *sukena nidra maya anubhuyate* – I slept very well. Therefore I am beyond the mind. You should know that you have a mind and you are beyond the mind. For some people they are the mind. It is as foolish as saying I am the shadow. You are not the shadow. The shadow is mine but I am not the shadow. This dress is mine, but I am not the dress. If you cannot understand this, then I will give you another example. The donkey is mine, but I am not the donkey. For strange reasons, that I do not know, everyone understands this example very well.

The mind is mine, but I am not the mind. So I am beyond the mind. I tell you when *gnanam* – understanding takes place you transcend the mind. When you transcend the mind, you are in a state of Samadhi – deep yogic absorption. Once you are in a state of *Samadhi*, the mind will not disturb you. *Yatra yatra mano yati tatra tatra samadhayaha.* This means you have a mind; let your mind go anywhere; you are in a state of Samadhi, but you should know something that is beyond the mind. If you are only the mind you get stressed. People take ganja, hashish, cocaine, krack and ecstasy; as you can see, I am up to date with all the drugs even though I have not taken any drugs. Do you know why people take all these? The mind is burdened and to relieve the burdened mind, people resort to drugs. Once you take drugs your thoughts become dull. Please don't do that. Understand that with meditation one can reach beyond this state.

So, the first is to understand the mind, the second is to transform the mind, and the third is to transcend the mind.

In the Bhagavad Gita Lord Krishna says, *"yagnanām aham japa yagnaha"*. It means that of all the yagnas, of all the sadhanas, I am *japa yagnaha*. He says, "I am japa". But lots of people do japa by way of murmuring without experiencing silence.

Soon you will realize, "Hey, I will not entertain negative thoughts. The moment I entertain negative thoughts it creates tension in my body. Why should it create tension in my body and mind? God has given me difficulties to humble me and not to tumble me. I need not worry." Worry is like a rocking-chair, it keeps you busy and leads you nowhere.

The whole of Lord Shiva's posture is the tapas posture. *Sa tapo tapyata sa tapas taptva tapo brahmeti dwijanat* — Lord Shiva is called Tapo tapyata — his posture is tapas, by tapas you have to understand brahma. And what is tapas? Tapas is to understand the mind, transform the mind, and transcend the mind.

The next time you find yourself worrying or your boss scolds you, practice tapas and have no negative thoughts. Don't say anything to your boss but practice within yourself. Tell yourself, "I will become tougher, maybe what he is saying is right and if he is wrong it is his mistake." Thus, if you start practicing, it will start happening, and the mind becomes a mantra. Once the mind becomes a mantra, the vibration of such a person has a tremendous impact all around. I have told you the story of the Shiva bhakta, whose shadow blesses the people, wherever he goes. He will not bless anyone because he is aware that he is no one to bless.

I am talking right now but I have not created the voice. How can I say that I am talking? Have I created this voice? If I am bringing in the right sloka am I putting my finger in the memory to do spiritual fingering? I am not doing anything for the memory but it is happening. Really I am not doing anything. I have told you a beautiful story from Shiva purana, about how Shiva bhakta – disciple does not bless, but his shadow blesses. If you really practise the meaning of this story, it would bring about spiritual energy. So what is the energy, which people have right now?

All of you can see, right now, that in the Kali Yuga people are very money-minded. I have analysed why this is so. Nowadays, people eat a lot in hotels. Earlier, there were no hotels and people did not eat out. Nowadays you see that everyone hosts a party in a hotel. If you give a party at home the food is brought from a hotel or it is cooked by the servants. Why the food cooked by your mother the most delicious food? It can never be equated with any other food, because when she cooks, her energy is so pure that the food she prepares is soaked with the vibration of her love. It is not a simple teaching, but the truth.

That is why breastfed children grow up to be healthier than the kids who drink packed milk. There are some mothers who don't breast feed their babies in order to take care of beauty. You know what happens as a result? Their children do not look after them later in their lives. Similarly, everywhere you go now, you have to eat hotel food. What is the wrong with hotel food? It is prepared to make money and not to make you happy. When you eat food made with the purpose of making money, all your energy goes into the idea of making money. When you get married you want to make money with your wife. Do you get what I am trying to elaborate?

Here is another story from Shiva Purana. Digest this story and you may understand the words 'chittam mantraha'.

There was a Shiva bhakta — devotee who was meditating under a tree. *Kaupina vanta khalu bhagyavanthaha* — with simple underwear he was very blissful. One day, a king was passing by. He was attracted by the bhakta's beautiful being and invited him to come and stay in his palace. The Shiva bhakta left his spot under the tree and went to the palace. There the King offered him his own room to stay. Food was served

to him. The next day he was to return. When he was
about to go back, he saw a beautiful necklace on the
king's bed. It was a very expensive necklace. The story
goes that he robbed the necklace, even though he knew
he was not doing the right thing, that too being a
jangama – jangama means Shiva bhakta.

All the same, he took it telling himself that when the
King had so much there was nothing wrong if he took
one necklace. He knew that if he asked the king, the king
would definitely give it to the jangama, the Shiva bhakta.
So, he told himself, there was no need to inform the
King. With such justification he took away the necklace.

When he went back to his abode, he began to eat the
ashram – hermitage food and suddenly he felt guilty. He
understood that what he had done was not the quality
of a Shiva bhakta; he chanted mrutyunjaya mantra and
did tapas.

He went back to the King and confessed that being a
jangama he had done such a thing. The king who was
also a good devotee could not believe it. The necklace
meant nothing to the King. So he made enquiries. What
type of food had been served to the jangama? The cook
was summoned, and the cook said that food of good
quality had been served. He was asked from where he had
got the ingredients? The cook replied that on that

particular day, some robbers were running away with several bags of rice stolen from the palace. When they saw some soldiers they dropped the bags of rice and ran away. The cook took the bags of rice back to the kitchen and used that rice to cook the meal. Then the king understood that the rice stolen by the robbers had given out that oorjha and that energy had gone into the food, which the jangama ate, and therefore the 'robbing energy' got better off him.

Don't take this example very lightly. This is why when we eat food we utter *brahmarpanam brahmahavihi…* we do *prokshana,* offer water on the food itself. We do not know what negative forces have gone into cooking the food. We can see for ourselves that the food prepared by our mother is very, very different because it is made with the purest of love. Therefore, by eating in the hotel, people have turned very money-minded.

What we eat is also very important. Because, the mental state of a person, who prepares food, has indirect impact on his preparation. Hence, *chittam mantraha.*

After cooking the food what do we do? We offer it to the Lord with an intension of purifying the food. Before eating the food, we do *prokshana* to all items that are being served. If you don't do *prokshana,* at least sincerely pray before eating. All these matter because when we eat, we

not only eat food, we also take in the vibration of the
people who prepared food.

Even the speaker gets charged, when there is a good
receptive audience. When there is a highly negative
audience, the speaker also gets drained. I am not exag-
gerating; at one point of time the highest rate of suicide
among professionals, was with psychiatrists. Listening
regularly to depressed people makes them depressed.
That is why psychiatrists have to go to other counselors
and pay a hefty fee to learn the art of listening and
meditation.

Once, a pretty girl went to a psychiatrist and
told him that she was full of tension. The
psychiatrist got up, hugged her and kissed her
and then sat down. She asked him why he did that. The
psychiatrist said that now that he had released his
tension, she could tell him what her tension was.

This is what happens, please understand. Even as a
speaker I can tell you that if the audience is very good
and receptive, we get charged – because there is vibration.
So, *chittam mantraha*.

Whenever you are free, please chant the mantra. Chant
the mantra, not in a hurried way, but with understanding.

See the gap, see the silence. When you start doing this, it would create a vibration; then when you go out, your energy would start blessing. You should always be available to observe the vibration.

I am trying my best to unfold the Shiva sutra in a condensed form. I don't want to burden you with too many sutras and so I am drawing out the essence of the sutras. You should be able to absorb it all.

Now, let us go further on Lord Shiva's symbol. What is it? It is Nandi – the bull which is in front of Lord Shiva. We have covered so many aspects of Lord Shiva. Each part of Lord Shiva – from the moon, to ganga, then the snake, the kamandalu, the japa mala, the trishula, the vibhuti, the third eye, the tiger skin – almost everything has been covered.

Nandi is the *vahana* – vehicle of Lord Shiva; it is always looking at Lord Shiva. When you go to a temple, you notice the Nandi in front of Lord Shiva, looking at Him constantly. It means Lord Shiva is generating tremendous energy but the bull is absorbing the energy. Sometimes you generate energy, and you don't know how to absorb it.

Have you seen some people giving love while some are

not able to receive love? I am using simple terms for you to understand. Some people can give a lot of love, but some cannot receive it. Some people can receive love but cannot give.

19

Mystery of Mystic

Reflect on this beautiful story from Zen literature.

A Zen Master was meditating under a tree for enlightenment and he generated such an energy field around him, that he created a new *shareera* - body. This has been described in Shiva sutra as *shareera utpattihi*. As he was sitting under the tree, the entire tree and the area were charged with such vibration, but still he was not enlightened. He felt miserable that he had done so much of tapas but still he was not enlightened. So, he left the place and went away thinking enlightenment was not his cup of tea.

Reflect on this story well. Along with the Shiva sutra, I am giving you all spiritual traps a *sadhaka* – seeker gets into. So you have to listen very attentively; if you miss even a minute, you will miss the whole thing.

When the Zen Master was meditating, he generated a body of vibration, armour around him. Still he was not enlightened. So he left the place and went away. It is said that a person who was not into meditation was passing by; he had a great capacity to absorb. When he looked at a flower, *avahanam samarpayami*, he was able to absorb. This may be because of his *poorva janma* – earlier birth; the tapas he had done in his previous birth.

The Zen Master could create the energy field, but was not able to absorb. When this person was casually walking in the forest, he navigated intuitively, as he was attracted to the magnetic energy field. The Zen Master had been meditating under the tree but went away. The field was charged, and this non-meditator had a tremendous capacity to absorb. Without any specific reason he sat under the tree where the Zen master had been meditating and for no particular reason he just closed his eyes... and the Zen story says that he became enlightened.

What a wonderful story this is! If you go through spirituality you will understand. This man was enlightened, where the Zen master had created the energy field, but he did not have the capacity to absorb it, whereas this man had the capacity to absorb.

Lord Shiva is a source of tremendous energy field. The Shiva bhakta is also a source for tremendous energy field. The Shiva Bhakta like Shiva's vahana – the bull, absorbs His energy. Therefore, another lesson you have to learn from the symbol of Shiva is to absorb.

If you are a true bhakta, even from a drunkard, you will learn never to be like a drunkard. You can learn from every situation in life. Dattatreya had 24 gurus. He learnt from everyone because he had the capacity to absorb. Some sadhakas are good at creating energy fields but they do not know how to absorb it. It is another invisible trap.

Therefore, in the symbol of Lord Shiva there is a powerful mystic energy field, but now we are focusing on Nandi – the bull that always faces Shiva. Are you able to absorb? You are listening to me now, there is an energy field right now, but if your mind is not *chittam mantraha*, you will not be able to absorb.

This could be one of the many reasons why Duryodana was not able to absorb Lord Krishna. Shakuni was not able to absorb Lord Krishna.

When you visit Lord Shiva's temple, you should be able to absorb each part of Lord Shiva. You should be like the bull always facing or absorbing the energy field. Once you know this, you will be able to absorb any energy field you encounter.

Hence, merely generating a positive energy field is not enough. One should be able to really absorb it. When one is able do this and chants Om Namah shivaya – generate the energy and absorb the energy then such a Shiva bhakta is *kaupina vanthaha khalu bhagyavanthaha.* He may have simple underwear, but *khalu bhagyavanthaha* – he is really blessed because for him *gnanam annam.* This understanding itself is *annam* – food.

This is another sutra – Understanding itself is *annam.*

I narrate another story, which will entertain you as well as enlighten you – please digest. Every example I give is loaded with meaning. Please absorb everything. Don't stop at laughing.

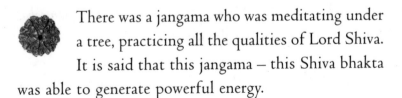 There was a jangama who was meditating under a tree, practicing all the qualities of Lord Shiva. It is said that this jangama – this Shiva bhakta was able to generate powerful energy.

A King saw this man under the tree who seemed to be

richer than those in the palace. The people in the palace were not happy like him. His eyes were luminous, and his presence was aesthetic. He was chanting the mantra and it appeared as if every cell of his being was dancing with positive vibration. So, the King could feel the energy of the vibration every time he passed by. It was like the perfume, the fragrance of those who have just had their bath. You smell the fragrance as you pass by them. Similarly, if you pass a person who smokes, you get the stink. A really spiritual person will have a spiritual perfume around him.

The jangama was wearing only simple underwear, but was in a state of ecstasy. The king requested him to come and stay in the palace and sanctify the palace. He brought him to the palace, gave him clothes to wear and asked him to stay there.

There was a belief that the vaasthu – energy field of a palace changes if a jangama stayed there. The sadhu started to wear the clothes he was given. They were like a king's dress with a small crown. He wore the clothes and also the crown. He ate from a golden plate and drank from a silver cup. Suddenly the king began to wonder whether this man was really a sadhu. The king himself had invited him to stay and given him clothes to wear.

Now, when the man started to use these luxuries the

King began to have doubts. He wondered if he had got the wrong person because according to his belief a sadhu should not touch gold and silver. For a week the sadhu stayed there and enjoyed all the luxuries offered by the king. All the time, the king wondered if he had brought the wrong person.

Lord Krishna says in the Bhagavad Gita, "*samshayatma vinashyati*" – the doubting man will perish. Once you begin to doubt, whatever others say you will not listen.

Mullah Nasruddin's wife had a doubt about Mullah. In the office his secretaries were all young girls. When the husband came home the wife would first check his coat. One day, she found a strand of hair on the coat. She thundered, "My God, you are having an affair with a girl". Mullah said, "I cannot afford an affair; isn't one affair enough for this janma?" "No, you men are naughty when you become forty, because you become haughty" was her argument. She did not believe him. The next day when her husband came home she checked his coat again. This time, she found a grey hair.

"My God, you are having affair with an old woman too." "No, I am not having any affair; this is too much I tell you" he retorted angrily. Again, she did not believe him. The next day Mullah applied another strategy. He cleaned the coat properly before entering the house. He went home confidently and hung up his coat. The wife searched the coat for evidence and found nothing. Immediately she screamed at the top of her voice, "You are having an affair with a bald woman". This is too much... *samshyatma vinashyati*.

We see in the above example, that the king brought this poor jangama to the palace, gave him all the luxuries, and the man was enjoying himself. I told you he was simple, but simplicity does not mean physical simplicity or simplicity in lifestyle. Therefore, he stayed. Then the King asked the Jangama, "What is the difference between you and me?" The Jangama said, "I would tell you tomorrow."

All night the King could not sleep. The next morning, they went for a walk. While they were walking, the King was anxious and the Jangama was relaxed. They were walking near the border of the kingdom; on the other side of the border was the land of the King's enemies. The King asked him to stop and said, "What is the upadesha, the message? The Jangama said, "Come let us walk". The King said, "That is the boundary of my kingdom and on the other side is the enemy. I have to stop; I cannot go on. I am the king only within this boundary." And the Jangama said, "This is the difference between you and me. You are limited by the boundary of your kingdom. I am not limited by any limitation."

Ishavashyam idhagum sarvam — "I see that Lord Shiva is everywhere but you are bound. You have limitations and I am not restricted by any limitations, because the Lord is limitless in His glory. You have an enemy in the opposite kingdom; I have none. Crossing the boundary means nothing to me. I can sit under the tree or stay in the palace. I can be on the other side of the boundary. Thus, you can see the difference between you and me. You are bound by your own territory, but for me God's boundary is my territory and God's territory has no boundaries."

Tears flowed out of the King's eyes. Many times, people listen to nice bhajans, but feel nothing; no tears flow. But the King wept for the Jangama — Lord Shiva's devotee had spoken a profound truth.

Adi Shankaracharya said, "*Yogaratov bhogaratov sangaratov sangaviheenah yasya brahmani ramate chittam nandati nandati nandati eva*". A real bhakta is one who remains unaffected in yoga and in bhoga; is *sangaratov* in the midst of people, *sangaviheenah* without any people; *brahmani ramate chittam* means his mind was revelling in Brahma. What is Brahma? *Satyam gnanam anantham brahma* — anantha means limitless. God is limitless. You are living in God's world, but you live with a personal agenda created by the

illusion that you are a king. Our identity itself is one
of the greatest illusions.

Sometime back, a leading newspaper had brought out an
article showing that the identity that we have of ourselves is an illusion. It is a pure Vedantic concept. Some
scientists have even said that the identity we have of
ourselves, is all an illusion. It is all a movement of
electrons and neutrons. For instance, we call this a moustache, pointing at one's moustache. Where is it written
that it is a moustache? We have branded it and marketed
it as a moustache. If I call the moustache, a beard, you'll
feel that Swamiji doesn't know English. Thus, the
identity itself is the illusion.

The great Saint Ramana said, *'Mana santu kim itu margane
krite naivamanasam marga arjavat'*. If you understand what
the mind is, then the mind does not exist at all. Like the
jangama who said, "I have no boundary, you have
boundaries."

The King had tears in his eyes and requested the jangama
to enlighten him. The jangama told the King to come
and sit down, at the boundary of his kingdom. The
teaching takes place at that boundary and the boundary
teaches us to learn to live as if the next moment would
bring death.

We are all seated on the boundary – where the next
moment can be death.

King Parikshith – the grandson of Arjuna, knew he was
going to die. He said, "I have seven days more, and I want
to learn right now from Sukhdev; I want to be enlightened. I want to attain *nirvana* – enlightenment". That
is how the Bhagavad was created and Sukhdev sat down
and taught the Bhagavad and thus King Parikshith was
enlightened.

The next moment could be death. Don't ever believe
your horoscope. That is another big illusion; instead
believe that the next moment can be death. Therefore,
seated at the boundary, the jangama teaches the king,
that there is no other boundary, and the only boundary
is death. The sutra he teaches is *vitharka atmagnanam*. I
cannot go into this sutra now as it requires a good deal
of unfoldment.

Vitharka atmagnanam. There are three types of logic - *tharka,
kutharka, vitharka.* Tharka is dry stupid knowledge – *"Na
tharkena aa paniya"*, say the Vedas. You cannot understand
everything by logic. You can understand only to some
extent. *Kutharka* is justifying logic.

"Why are you miserable?" I asked someone. "If you work
in our organisation, then you'll know why I am

miserable." People justify and we use logic to justify. This is called *kutharka*. *Vitharka* means breakthrough logic. Your logical thinking should have a breakthrough; you should convert a breakdown into a breakthrough. That is what is practiced in management.

In spirituality, our breakdown is in a state of *samsara*. *Samsara* means deficiency. We are always a "wanting being", so you must have a breakthrough from the state of being... a "wanting being".

20

Grace – Graceful way of Inner Unfoldment

How can I attain *nirvana*? The jangama says, '*Vitharka atmagnanam*'. What is *Atmagnanam*? Atma means self, so find out who you are. How do you find out who you are? 'I will find out who I am. I will store this knowledge for the next birth, and then I will practice it.' No, that is kutharka.

Vitharka means right now be with the question. *Asmin kshane* – right now the boundary of the enemy, the boundary of death is *atmagnamam*. Don't get lost in *tharka*, *kutharka*, or *vitharka*; most of us are lost in *kutharka*. Most of us, especially the educated audience, are very good at *kutharka*. "Swamiji, you are a sadhu, it is Ok for you, but

we are *samsaris*." Who asked you to be a *samsari*? *Samsari*
is a state of mind, and has nothing to do with dress. If
this dress can make you a Swamiji, then put it on a
buffalo. Will it become a Swamiji? Our dress is to remind
us of what we have to be.

Therefore, please understand right now, *atmagnanam*. The
jangama teaches the king, "Right now, who are you? Are
you this body?" Let me not elaborate too much. Please
listen very attentively. If you have punya you will understand; if you don't have punya that is a manufacturer's
defect.

This body is *drishyam* — means seen. You are the *drik* —
means seer. This is what the jangama was teaching the
King — body is *dhrishyam* — means seen and the self is the
seen or the seer.

It has to be the Seer. What is seen is the object. The Seer
alone is the self. In Sanskrit 'self' is called Atma. Is the
body the Seen or the Seer?

It is the Seen.

If the body is the Seen, then 'I' cannot be the body. I
am the Seer. Then, "Who am I?"

"I am the mind". The mind is also the Seen — *dhrishyam*.

Mind is thought and thought is seen. So how can you be the mind? You are seeing the thought. So thoughts are seen, I am the Seer. The Self is the Seer. Atma means self. Thoughts are seen, so then who am I? I cannot be the thought, for it is seen and I am the seer. Then "Who am I?"

"I am the intellect", Swamiji.

"Why?"

"I am a doctor".

"Were you born with intellectual knowledge and knowledge of medicine? Is any doctor born with such knowledge?"

"No, my knowledge was acquired".

If it is acquired then you are the acquirer acquiring the acquired. So you are not the acquired, you are the acquirer – means you are the Seer, so you cannot be the doctor. You were not born with ophthalmologic knowledge; you acquired it. Who is the person who acquired it? "He is the self". You are not the body because it is seen, you are not the thought because it is seen, and you are not the knowledge because it is seen.

"Swamiji, definitely you cannot neglect me; I am ignorant, because I am ignorant of what you are talking. So I am ignorant".

"So how do you know you are ignorant?"

"Because I know that I do not know".

So if you know that you don't know, are you ignorant? Because you know that you don't know. So therefore you are not ignorant. Then, "Who are you?"

"Ultimately what is the *siddhanta* or essence, Swamiji? I am *shoonya* – empty".

If you are *shoonya*, *shoonya* cannot say that it is *shoonya*. There must be some presence saying I am *shoonya*. So you cannot be *shoonya*. Then who are you? This is where you have to see the self. That is what the jangama said.

To begin with, you say you are not the body but the body is yours; you are not the mind but the mind is yours. "I am not the shirt but the shirt is mine; I am not the knowledge but the knowledge is mine. I am not ignorance but the ignorance is mine. So who am I?"

"See what you are not, which you have taken as yours –

this is called *nethi nethi...* negate, negate. I am not the body, I am not the mind, and I am not the thought. Now you have negated that which is seen – I am not the body, who is seeing, I am not the mind, who is seeing; now see that seer, which is seeing the seeing".

"See that seer". The great Ramana Maharishi says that up to here you and I do *sadhana* – spiritual practice. Up to here, I am not the body, but body is mine. Even the great Ramana Maharishi says I am not all these that I have taken as mine. So first remove the misunderstanding and see, "Who is that person?" – be there in that question. Ramana Maharishi says that you and I can come up to this point. Afterwards, it is *Jai Bhajaranga Bali*. Ramana Maharishi says that after this point only grace can take you to the next level.

Only grace can take you to the next level. When that happens, *Vitharka atmagnanam* up to this point, and afterwards it depends on your guru's blessings, the Lord's blessings. Therefore, this Jangama says *Vitharka atmagnanam* – you are not the body, you are not the mind, you are not the emotion, you are not the intellect; please don't make the mistake of thinking that if you are not the body it means you should not care for the body. Understand what is being said, the body is mine but I am not the body, the shadow is mine but I am not the shadow, the house is mine, but I am not the house. Get the clarity.

Or else everything becomes a matter of mine, mine, mine and the neighbour's wife is also mine. For some, 'anything and everything is mine', they say. And then they say *vitharka atmagnanam*; the story goes that at that moment the boundary becomes enlightenment.

Therefore, if you are really a Shiva bhakta, every moment when you do japa, absorb each part of Lord Shiva like a bull. And when you absorb all these qualities, you would have prepared wonderful spiritual soil; having prepared the soil, just wait. When the great blessings dawns, when the grace happens, you will not know and therefore *Chittam Mantraha – vitharka atmagnanam*. But that *vitharka atmagnanam* would happen when you stop poisoning yourself each moment.

Worry – An
Inner Poisoning

Visham thyajet – what is *visham thyajet*? We did see this earlier. *Visham* is poison or poisonous food; *thyajet* means to give away – you should give away poisonous food. You should learn to give away poisonous food. If you don't give away the poisonous food then with the poisonous food, even the best of seeds sowed in it will not sprout. It will be like the unfertilised soil.

Visham thyajet – avoid poisonous food. Now what is poisonous food? Think quickly. There is poisonous food for the body – eating wrong food is poisonous food. First you should stop such food for the body. Next, what state are you keeping your body in? What is the state?

If you are keeping your body restless, or tense, it is poison for your body.

In the Bhagavad Gita, Lord Krishna tells Arjuna in the battlefield, "*Prasannachetaso hyāsu buddhih paryavatisthate*" – Be cheerful and fight, O Arjuna". It means keep your body in a happy state. That is good food for your body.

When you do yogasana and pranayama, you generate positive energy in the body. The more you keep the body cheerful, happy and relaxed, sharper will be certain receptors in the body. You would soon realize that the right type of food is not poisonous food, your sense organs would become extremely sharp, so too, your intuitive ability. You need that acumen and it must build up in your body.

So, the first discipline we must learn is easy – all of you must smile. If you are a Shiva bhakta, smile. That is why all the Gods are gently smiling seeing our stupidity.

One day a Father was teaching the students how to give a speech; when you talk about heaven your face should be like heaven, when you talk about love, it should be radiating love. Another father asked, 'what about when I talk about hell'. 'Your ordinary face itself is enough', said the former.

Why youngsters are not turning spiritual? They see their parents in a pensive mood always; if you cannot smile, you cannot enjoy things.

Once I visited a place in Rajasthan, where everybody claimed that they have become enlightened. I looked at their faces; they all had a look of a constipated person suffe-ring from piles. I thought to myself that if this is enlightenment, I don't want enlightenment. My ordinary state is enough. The word 'enlightenment' has become so polluted.

A politician noticed that a lot of youngsters had become disciples of a particular guru. The politician asked the youngsters what is it that is in the guru's face to inspire them to leave their home and follow him. The students said, 'when we see our guru's face, we know God exists'. The politician asked them what they understand from looking at his face. They said, 'Even God can make mistakes'.

Don't think I am talking high-level psychology now. Lord Krishna says it in the Bhagavad Gita – *Prasanna Chetasa*. So the first thing to do is, if you are really a bhakta and spiritual seeker, being cheerful and keep your face cheerful. Don't give the plastic smile, in the earlier example, as if you are about to say, 'Thank you for flying with Lufthansa'. Look really cheerful.

After all, you are a bhakta of the Lord. You may ask why you should be cheerful. Please tell me, if you and I were to create the sun, how many billions of years would it take us? If you and I were to create the stars or the flora and the fauna, how many billions of years would it take us? All these are the miracles, the ecstasy of this creation. If you and I were to chisel the sun, chisel the stars, chisel the galaxy, it would take us billions and billions of years. And God has given us this buffet of ecstasy free of cost. Looking at this buffet of ecstasy, my God, you should say *Jai Bhajaranga Bali*. So, just be happy. Even if your husband leaves you, don't worry, if one idiot goes another idiot will come. You will never be disappointed with any affair.

I am not talking in the loose sense of the term; I am speaking in a very different sense of the term. See the context; don't catch my words. If you catch my words I have already passed my words.

Therefore, it is said, *Visham thyajet*. Therefore, smile. But not to be cheerful is like poison.

Secondly, have you seen so many tense people? I ask people to sit down, but their legs will be shaking, constantly shaking. We find that there is no silence around them. Have you seen some people eating food, they just gulp it.

In Indian tradition, we have something called *Anna Poorneshwari Upasana*. Eating food is like meditation. In one of my programmes, we teach participants how to eat their food: how to eat food meditatively. When you eat, you should do so with a lot of bhakti, and you should be relaxed. Keep your body graceful. Eat food gracefully.

If I am using my hand it should be relaxed. Every part of your body should be relaxed. Not being relaxed is being tense. It is poison. So, it is *visham thyajet*. Drop all poisonous emotions. I mentioned earlier about jealousy and attachment. People develop attachment – it can be very natural or even cultivated. They come to the ashram and become attached to the guru also.

Once, a man came from New York to Bombay to get married. He met a girl whom he liked and decided he would marry her. He gave a beautiful diamond ring and visa papers and they decided that they would get married after 6 months. After 6 months, he came back to get married and could hardly recognise the girl. "This is not the girl I wanted to get married to."

"No. I was practicing to eat like a typical American. Pizza for breakfast, burger for lunch, and spaghetti in between", said the girl.

"I don't want to get married to you, give back my ring",
he demanded.

"Ok, take the ring." But the ring did not come off her
finger. He tried and tried but no success. Then he said,
"Forget it, I will marry you." What for? Just for the sake
of the ring.

So, drop all negative emotion. Therefore, drop the
poison *visham thyajet*...whether it is poison for the body,
poison for the mind or poison for the intellect. What
is the poisonous food for the mind? Again, it is the
restless mind. A restless mind is poisonous food for the
mind. The mind is always restless.

To worry is to insult God's wisdom. "Develop your
Shakti", says Lord Shiva. What has to happen would
happen.

Most of our worries and tensions come from our
conditioning. The greatest poison of our mind is our
conditioning. Maybe you don't realise it. I touch on this
in my LIFE programme. We are all victims of conditioning. That is why some people are confused to learn
that I have cats and dogs in my ashrams. They wonder
how a Swamiji can have cats and dogs. A journalist asked,
"Arrey, Swamiji has cats and dogs" and writes an article

about it. See how the conditioning happens.

I would like to tell you an incident involving the controversial guru Osho Rajneesh. I love this incident. Osho Rajneesh was a very mischievous guru and also a wise person. Once when he was traveling by train in North India, a lot of devotees came to garland him. An orthodox Pandit watched all those people garlanded this mystic with a long beard and came into Rajneesh's first class compartment and sat down. The Pandit thought he was very lucky to share the compartment with the sadhu and felt happy. He touched Rajneesh's feet saying that it was a great blessing for him to be traveling with such a big guru. Osho was a mischievous guru. Here, was an orthodox Pandit touching his feet. He asked him, "Do you know who I am?" "I know you are a Mahatma." Osho said, "No, I am a Sufi Fakir." Immediately, this man turned to go away to wash his hands because he had touched a Muslim's feet. Osho said, "I am only joking, I am a Hindu monk." The Pandit quickly said, "I knew it from your eyes and the luster in your face" and again he touched Osho's feet. Now Osho spoke seriously, "Ok, now I am not joking. I am a Sufi Fakir" and this drama went on for some time. Tell me, how does it matter if you are a Muslim, Christian or Hindu?

So what?

See how conditioning plays a role. Just observe yourself.
See your conditioning influences you. You have to learn
to drop all conditioning. The greatest poison is our
conditioning. Saint Kabir says, "*Hadh hadh per sabhee gaye
behad gayana koi behadh ke maidan me mein kabira soi*".
Everybody is living within boundaries (*Hadh hadh per sabhee
gaye*), in the boundaryless existence without boundary
there is no conditioning (behadh gayana koi); it appears
people are not reveling, only Kabir seems to be reveling
(mein Kabira soi).

Hence, we must make an effort to drop all our
conditioning. Stop poisoning the body, stop poisoning
the mind, stop poisoning the emotion. When you drop
all these poisons – *visham thyajet* happens. And when you
drop the *visham*, then you would experience *vitarka
atmagnanam*. Because you are in the best possible soil and
the seeds can be sown. The seeds would not have
sprouted in unfertile soil. "*Visham thyajet vitarka
atmagnanam*". And to do that, practice *chittam mantraha*.

22

Fragrance of Inner Surrender

Always remember, *gnanam annam* and for it to happen *Shakti sandhane shareera utpattihi*. What is meant by Shakti? – We have elaborated on *Ichcha Shakti, Vidya Shakti and Kriya Shakti.*

When a wild flower grows in the forest, nobody recognizes the flower, nobody waters the flower, nobody admires its beauty, nobody thanks the flower, for is the flower not silently and gently contributing to the ecstasy of the forest?

Isn't it true that nobody thanks the flower although the flower is silently contributing? Let our life be like a flower; to continue doing, to contribute whether people recognise it or not. The flower contributes to the forest.

Whenever you offer a flower to Lord Vishnu or Lord
Shiva, the *bilva patra,* flower you offer with a beautiful
sloka. If you practice this wonderful piece of wisdom,
your life would change.

*"Ahimsa prathamam pushpam, pushpam indriya nigraham,
sarvabhoota daya pushpam, kshama pushpam visheshata, shanti
pushpam tapo pushpam, dhanam pushpam tataiyacha, satyam
astavidam pushpam vishuho preeti karambhavet."*

Preeti karambhavet means whatever flower is valuable
or pleasing to the Lord, is the flower which is offered.
When you offer the flower, it has many petals and each
petal gives out fragrance and this will be the flower
which is really valuable to the Lord. *Ahimsa prathamam
pushpam* – ahimsa means non-injury; if you are really a
bhakta you do not injure others or yourself. Don't
practice non-injury to a ridiculous extent. For instance,
there are some who do not even touch an ant. Basically,
the intention should be not to injure anybody. That is
why Sanyasis take a vrata – stand at the time of taking
Sanyas. *Sarva Bhootepyaha abhayam datwa naiskaryam achare*
is the vrita we take. To all beings (Sarva Bhootepyaha)
I give non-injury (abhaya dhanam); I am not lost in
activity (naishkaryam) but we are in action (acharet).
Don't forget the distinction between activity and action.

ahimsa prathamam pushpam — the first flower is *ahimsa* — don't injure yourself and don't injure others.

Pushpam indriya nigraham — the second flower is *indriya nigraham* — develop self-control. *Indriya nigraham* is the second flower that Vishnu, the Lord, likes. Let us develop mastery. There is tremendous joy in self-control.

Sarva bhoota daya pushpam — *dhaya* means 'be kind'. What is kindness? There is so much of injustice based on which religion, which *jathi* a person belongs to. If one is a widow, one is treated badly. In our culture widows are treated very badly. The whole division is because of lack of kindness. Yet, in the Vishnupurana, it is said very clearly — *sarva bhoota dhaya pushpam*.

Kshama pushpam visheshataha — kshama means forgiveness, *visheshataha* means you should know how to forgive. Forgiveness is the fourth flower that the Lord wants us to bring forth.

Shanti pushpam, tapo pushpam — *shanti* means peace, *tapo* means *tapas*, *dhyanam pushpam* — *dhynam* means meditation. Therefore, shanti pushpam tapo pushpam, dhyanam pushpam tataivacha.

Satyam ashtavidam pushpam — *satyam* means to be truthful, *ashtavidam pushpam* — means the eight types of flowers.

Vishnoho preeti karambhavet. "This pleases me, said Lord Vishnu."

Be honorable; be authentic in life for *sathyam astavidam pushpam vishnoho preeti karambhavet.*

This is the kind of flower you should offer to the Lord. Once you offer this kind of flower, the blessings are not only showered on you but also on your family. I want you to do the homework of digesting and practicing this.

The King, referred in the previous example, asked the Jangama, 'who his family members were?' The Jangama, the Shiva bhakta said, '*Satya Mata Gnana* Pitha Dharma Bhratha Daya guruhu, shanti mitram kshama bhratru, shadehe mamo bhandavaha, shadehe *mamo bandhavaha*'. The jangama said that these six (shadehe) are my relatives (mama bandhavaha).

Satya mata — truth is my mother.

My mother is not my biological mother, but truth.

Gnana pitha — clarity is my father;

dharma bhratha — dharma is my brother;

daya guruhu — kindness is my guru;

shanti mitram — silence is my *mitra*, my friend;

kshama bhratru — forgiveness is my sister,

shadehe mama bandhavaha — these six are my relatives.

23

The Unquenching Thirst

I will answer few of your questions.

Q: How does 'Om' impact the body and mind?

A: When you are chanting any mantra, and especially Om, it creates a certain vibration. When you chant, please observe that it should be through both inhalation and exhalation. The mouth should be half open and half closed. Above the palate is the pituitary and above the pituitary is the hypothalamus, the master glands of the endocrine system. The head has a concave shape, which creates a pyramid-like effect. Your pituitary gland and hypothalamus are covered with a pyramid-like effect. So when you are chanting it impacts your pituitary and hypothalamus.

Thus, the chanting charges the hypothalamus and the pituitary, which are the master glands of your endocrine system; and the chemical balance within you is changed.

Remember chanting can reduce most of our tension and depression. I would like you to understand that every cell in the nervous system sends a message through a cell called axon and receives the message through the cell called dendrite; between these two cells is synoptic fluid. And in this synoptic fluid you have dopamine and serotonin. When you become tense your dopamine and serotonin levels get disturbed. When they are disturbed, if a cell sends a message through axon, which is received through dendrite, the transmission is very foggy. This mental fogginess is transmitted to your brain and therefore your perception becomes foggy.

That is why when people suffer from depression, they are given a dopamine pill. When you take a dopamine pill, the dopamine level is back to normal; alternatively, if you chant the mantra correctly, it impacts the pituitary and hypothalamus the master glands of the whole endocrine system, your synaptic fluid and dopamine, then there is harmony in your chemical balance. Thus, the message is transmitted from axon to dendrite very smoothly.

So, chanting a mantra is clinically proved to have an impact, because ultimately you and I are our chemistry. Even if a great soul, a noble person takes a high dose of cocaine or crack or ecstasy, he would behave in an imbalanced manner. You and I are chemistry. When you chant the mantra, the right chemistry is created in your body, and that chemistry has a deep impact.

Q: Is enlightenment possible, for one who is in samsara?

A: Enlightenment is possible only for such people. People who are not in samsara are already enlightened. It is a reality for them, not a possibility. Enlightenment is possible only for people in samsara. Therefore, please understand that you have to remove this misconception that only a monk or ascetic can achieve enlightenment.

In the Bhagavad Gita Lord Krishna tells Arjuna, '*Karmanyevahi samsiddhim astita janakaadaya*'. He quotes Janaka who was a great king. *Karmanyevahi samsiddhim* — by living a life of action, Janaka, the King engaged in action attains enlightenment.

Lord Krishna quotes Janaka, not Ashtavakra, who was Janaka's guru; therefore, we see that enlightenment is very much possible to those in samsara.

When you clap you produce a sound. To make that sound you have to put in an effort. When there is no sound, there is silence, and no effort. Therefore, to be in silence requires no effort. People who worry have many ways to be miserable. I have seen people being unhappy. I always say therefore, I have become enlightened not by reading the Shiva sutra, not by reading Bhagavad Gita, but just by looking at my students.

Many have attained enlightenment but to do so, you should have *Icchcha Shakti*, *Vidya Shakti* and *Kriya Shakti* and you should practice with understanding. Even if you are not enlightened, be very loving. Be happy, for even being in samsara is wonderful. If you have the knack of being happy, then even if your wife is bugging you, nagging you or your husband is dominating you, you can see the 'Wah, wah!' in life. But if you don't have the knack of being happy, then when your husband is dominating you, you are full of tension.

If your wife is nagging you, look at her communication skill – pause, pitch, punctuation, voice modulation, opening statement, closing statement, funnel technique, multiple closes, disarming technique and pre-emptive strike.

Q: *What is the purpose of life and how can one become a balanced person when there are ups and downs in one's life?*

A: I would like to elaborate through Zen philosophy. Life is empty and meaningless. The Zen master talks in puzzles. What is the purpose of life, somebody asked the Zen Master. He said that life is empty and meaningless. When I say empty and meaningless, please understand that it is not useless. It means that life is like an empty canvas, the canvas has no meaning, but the canvas provides a platform for you to write whatever you want to write.

When he says life is empty and meaningless, he means that the canvas is empty, and so has no meaning. So, what do you do on the empty canvas? You write God is love. That is the meaning you are giving to the canvas, to life. So life is an empty board and will have only whatever meaning you give to life; else life does not have purpose. Our Rishis said that enlightenment is the meaning of life. Underworld Dons and others say loot, hook or crook form the meaning of life; a terrorist would give another meaning. Thus, each one of us gives our own meaning to life. As such life as such has no meaning.

I will say two things. Be happy and do good.

If you don't want a complicated answer, I will tell it very

simply, be happy and do good.

How to be balanced is very important. In my LIFE
workshop I teach the participants how to be balanced.
Life is not just about being a doctor. Life is not just
about being a housewife. Life has various zones —
intimate zone, family zone, work zone, social zone, and
spiritual zone. You have to balance all the zones of your
life.

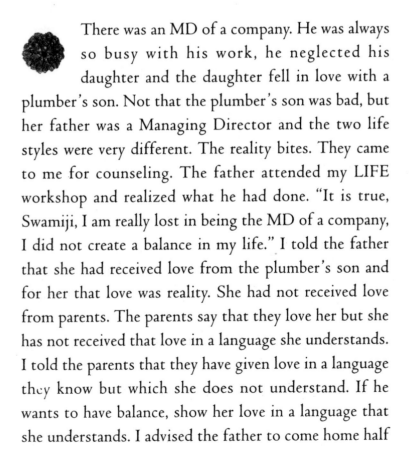There was an MD of a company. He was always
so busy with his work, he neglected his
daughter and the daughter fell in love with a
plumber's son. Not that the plumber's son was bad, but
her father was a Managing Director and the two life
styles were very different. The reality bites. They came
to me for counseling. The father attended my LIFE
workshop and realized what he had done. "It is true,
Swamiji, I am really lost in being the MD of a company,
I did not create a balance in my life." I told the father
that she had received love from the plumber's son and
for her that love was reality. She had not received love
from parents. The parents say that they love her but she
has not received that love in a language she understands.
I told the parents that they have given love in a language
they know but which she does not understand. If he
wants to have balance, show her love in a language that
she understands. I advised the father to come home half

an hour early from office. As an MD he is successful, but as a father he was an utter failure; his wife says that as a husband he was the worst husband.

So balance your intimate zone. Intimate means what is private. I am a Swamiji but I love sports. Only recently I stopped practicing martial arts. I love basketball. After becoming a Swamiji, I continued to play basketball, out of interest. Some people, who did not like it, asked me if it were written in the scriptures that I could play such games. Then I told them that if it is not written, please do write it in the scriptures. The scriptures do not go into details about what type of watch one should wear.

Sing your song; don't sing the song of your grandfather. In the evening of life you find you have not lived your life; you have lived only a proxy life. So balance your life.

Q: I lost my son when he was 25 years old. In the midst of all the tragedies that happened it appears that whatever I have done for him is totally futile when death takes away. I would like to know more about prarabdha and destiny. Please enlighten us, how we can accept this tragedy.

A: I understand your feeling that you have lost your son and you wonder how to accept it. First thing you should understand is the *shodasa samskaras* – 16 rituals a Hindu undergoes. The Indian thought is very profound. When you understand this, you will realise that when the child is born the karma is called *jata karma*. With a golden needle honey and milk are tipped on the tongue of the child and you gently write Om. Then you say, *"Vedosi ashma bhava parashar bhava"*. *Vedosi* – you are the child of the Veda, meaning you are not my child. You are child of the Veda. Right from the moment of birth, you say that the child is the child of the Lord, not my child. And therefore, what is the sloka given to you at the time of the birth of the child? *"Poojayet Panchavarshani dashavarshani dhandayet praptetu shodaashavarshe putram mitravat acharet"*.

Poojayet Panjavarshani – The parents are told to worship the child for 5 years; *dashavarshani* – from the age of 5 to 15, *dhandayet* create discipline; *praptetu shotashavarshe* - when the child reaches 16th year, *putram mitravat acharet* – treat the child as a friend. The child is no more a child.

So, right from the birth he is not your child. You must understand that you are only a trustee. When the child is born, it is not your child. Whatever years the child lives with you, understand that it is a great gift. And if you say the child is taken away, the Lord has taken away. The problem crops up when you take ownership of your child. But the fact is it is not your child. Not your child, don't hear it wrongly.

Look, when I am talking it is not really my voice. I have

not created this voice. I find myself with this voice. So whose voice is this? It is the Lord's voice. I have not created this brain; I find that the brain is working. So nothing is mine; everything is thine. When you understand that, you won't take ownership, but will only take trusteeship.

Lord Krishna says, *"Nimitta matram bhava"* – just be an instrument.

There is a beautiful episode in the life of Rukmini, wife of Lord Krishna. Lord Krishna always carried the flute. Rukmini, the wife of Lord Krishna, felt "The flute is so lucky for it is always with my beloved. I am married to him but not always with my beloved." The only time Lord Krishna was away from the flute was when he took a bath. One day, when Lord Krishna went for his bath, Rukmini praised the flute and performed pooja to the flute. The soul of the flute came out; and she asked the flute to tell her the secret and magic. The flute was with her beloved all the time although she was the wife of the Lord. And the flute said, "I don't know. All that I know is that I am totally empty that is why the music flows."

Rukmini became enlightened. Just be empty. To be close to the Lord, just be empty. Nothing is mine, everything is thine. Whatever I am given, I am only the trustee.

When you understand this, you would realise that even the few years your son lived with you was a wonderful period. Wah! What an experience. It is not the quantity of years that you have lived, it is the depth with which you lived your life that makes the difference. Learn to live life deeply. There are a lot of people who have multiple sexual experiences and still they are shallow. But there are those people who have experienced the flame of love just once and it has transformed them while those with multiple experiences remain shallow. So, it is not the quantity but the depth that matters.

A section of large crowd during Gita Talks by Swamiji

A view of Nirguna Mandir at Bangalore

51, Ground Floor, 16th Cross,
Between 6th & 8th Main
Malleswaram, Bangalore 560 055, India

Tel: +91 80 4153 5832-35
Fax: +91 80 2344 4112
E-mail: prasannatrust@vsnl.com
www.swamisukhabodhananda.org
www.prasannatrust.org
www.ohmindrelaxplease.org

Prasanna Trust is a registered social charitable trust set up with the objective to re-look at various facets of Indian philosophy and culture for effective transformation of individuals in particular and the society in general.

We have made our presence primarily through :

- Transformative Education
- Social Oriented Service

TRANSFORMATIVE EDUCATION

a) LIFE – LIVING IN FREEDOM – AN ENQUIRY

It is a 2 days workshop on personal effectiveness through interactions and meditations. An experience oriented, non-religious program designed to enhance productivity, handling stress, personal well-being and organisational synergy. It focuses on bringing forth the outer winner leading to creativity and an inner winner to meditative consciousness.

b) EXISTENTIAL LABORATORY

It is a 4-days residential retreat set amidst natural surroundings to experience oneself through a series of dynamic and passive meditations in order to see connectivity with nature, to heal and release the inner child, to realise innocence and wonderment in all walks of life based on the Upanishad truths – Chakshumathi Vidya.

c) CORPORATE HARMONY AND CREATIVITY

It is a 2 days comprehensive workshop for senior level executives to harness creativity and harmony in today's competitive work environment and preparing them for globalisation.

d) YOUTH PROGRAM

It is a 2 days program based on multiple intelligence. The program develops the hidden talent and skill in a child; to enable the child to face the world with confidence as each child is unique.

e) ART OF WISE PARENTING PROGRAM

It is a 1 day program on importance of Parenting –
Motivation, people skills, parenting as a learning
journey, to operate from openness. The program is
about – Is one a learning parent or a teaching parent?

f) OH, MIND RELAX PLEASE!

It is a 1 day seminar based on unique techniques to
transform from ordinary to extraordinary, dealing
with fear and conflicts and converting them as
challenges..

g) RELATIONSHIP MATRIX SEMINAR

An exclusive workshop to discover alchemy of
different spectrum of relationship, be it father,
mother, spouse, children, sibblings, boss, sub-
ordinate colleagues, associate peers..., so as to
discover togetherness in a relationship.

h) TEACHERS' TRAINING PROGRAM

A 5 days workshop designed to train and develop an
individual as Pracharak or teacher for spreading the
universal message for the benefit of society.

i) MANTRA YOGA PROGRAM – A Holistic approach to Life

A workshop based on five powerful Mantras to help in enhancing health, unlocking the blissful centre, increasing intuitive ability, creating wealth and divinity in oneself and others. This program is conducted in English and also in many Indian languages by well trained Pracharaks.

j) NIRGUNA MANDIR – A Meditation Centre for Learning

* Unfolding the traditional texts of the Bhagavad Gita & the Upanishads as is relevant in today's living context.

* Workshops to bring forth creativity and awareness among youth, women and parents through a spiritual paradigm.

* Research to foster universal love through an interreligious forum.

* Orientation programs for trainers and social workers.

* Spiritual inputs to deal with phobia, fear, trauma, drug and alcoholic abuse.

SOCIAL ORIENTED SERVICE

a) CHILD CARE CENTRE – A HOME FOR HOMELESS – PRASANNA JYOTHI:

Nurturing lives of little angels who have been orphaned due to the paradox of circumstances. Uncared girls who otherwise would have withered away are growing into enthusiastic, intelligent, celebrative and responsible children.

b) ARTIFICIAL LIMB CAMP : Providing support for mobility aids like calipers for deserving cases for the underprivileged with disability from impoverished background.

c) POOR FEEDING: Regular poor feeding for the poorest of the poor.

d) SCHOLARSHIP FOR MERITORIUS STUDENTS: This facility is extended to those who belong to economically weaker section, irrespective of caste, creed, color and religion.

Contribution to **Prasanna Trust** account is exempted from **Income Tax under Section 80 (G)**.

TITLES OF SWAMIJI'S WORKS
BOOKS

Oh, Mind Relax Please!
(also in Tamil, Telugu, Kannada, Malayalam, Hindi, Marathi & Gujarati)

Oh, Mind Relax Please! – Part 2 *(only in Tamil, Kannada & Telugu)*

Oh, Life Relax Please!
(also in Hindi, Tamil, Telugu, Kannada, Gujarati and Marathi)

Meditation *(from Bhagavad Gita)* *(also in Kannada, Tamil, Telugu & Hindi)*

Stress Management – A bullet proof Yogic Approach (also in Kannada & Hindi)

Art of Wise Parenting *(also in Kannada & Hindi)*

Looking at Life Differently *(also in Tamil, Telugu, Kannada, Hindi & Marati)*

Wordless Wisdom *(also in Tamil, Kannada, Hindi, Telugu & Marathi)*

Golden Words for Good Living

Karma Yoga *(based on Bhagavad Gita)* *(also in Kannada & Hindi)*

Roar Your Way to Excellence *(also in Kannada, Marathi, Hindi & Tamil)*

Celebrating Success & Failure *(also in Kannada & Tamil)*

Harmonising Inner Strength *(also in Kannada, Marathi &*
Hindi)
Personal Excellence through the Bhagavad Gita *(also in*
Kannada & Hindi)
Inspiring Thoughts for Harmonious Living
Agame Relax Please! *(in Tamil)*
Kutumbave Relax Please! *(in Kannada & Telugu)*
Elaignane Relax Please! *(in Tamil)*

AUDIO
TRADITIONAL UNFOLDMENT

Gayatri Mantra *(also in regional languages)*
Maha Mruthyunjaya Mantra *(also in regional languages)*
Om Gam Ganapateya Namaha *(also in regional languages)*
Om Krishnaya Namaha *(also in regional languages)*
Om Shivaya Namaha *(also in regional languages)*
Healing Hurt through Gayatri Mantra
Handling Insecurity through Mruthyunjaya Mantra
Handling Crisis through Taraka Mantra
Mantra Yoga (Gayatri Mantra)
Mantra Yoga (Mruthyunjaya Mantra)

MEDITATION

Mahavisarjana Kriya

Navratri Upasana

Bhakti Yoga

Mantra Healing

Trataka Yogic Technique

Brahma Yagna

Meditation – the Music of Silence

Vedic Vision to Pregnant Women

Yogalaya

Seven Chakras of Hindu Psychology

MANAGEMENT – A NEW LOOK THROUGHS SPIRITUAL PARADIGM

Self Confidence through Hypnosis

Essence of Hinduism

Symbolism of Hindu Rituals

How to Deal with Fear

Stress Management

People Management – an Enlightened Approach

Art of Wise Parenting

Creating a Happy Marriage

Hypnosis & Relationship

OCCULT TEACHINGS

LIFE Program – Living in Freedom – an Enquiry
Guru Purnima
Mantra Chants
Who am I?
Shiva Sutras
Gita Talks

BHAJANS

Bhajans with the Master (Vol. I)

VIDEO (in VCD form)

Get Rid of Stress – Stress Management through Spirituality
Jokes to Joy – Navarasas
Suffering to Surrender
Discouragement to Encouragement
Worry to Wisdom
Seeds of Wisdom
Looking Life Differently – Bhagavad Gita Chapter.5
A Balanced Man
Inner Awakening
Harmony in Chaos
Bhagavad Gita (Vol. I to 32)
Shiva Sutras (Vol. I to 8)

Swamiji's workshop empowers one to be Effective, Creative & Celebrative in all walks of life.

'LIFE' – a two-days workshop on how to use the mind for Success and Satisfaction

Objective of the Seminar:

Outer Winner

- The art of powerful goal setting.
- Decision-making, Team building.
- Divine principles of worldly achievement.
- Interpersonal skills & Effective communication
- How to deal with difficult people.
- Possibility thinker.

Inner Winner

- The art of being blissful, restful and loving.
- The art of healing psychological wounds.
- Mind management
- Worry management.
- Fear management.
- Meditation to bring about healthy inner healing and enlightenment.

What others say about the programme:

"Here's one Guru who's in tune with modern times."

– India Today.

"The unusual Swami from Bangalore is the latest Guru on the Indian Management scene."

– Business India.

True Freedom Lies
In the Art of Looking at Life Afresh

Glide through work pressures without the 'Sting of Stress'. Say Yes to Growth, Achievement, Progress Say No to Stress, Fatigue, Pressure.

Existential Laboratory
a four-day residential workshop

Amidst a carnival of natural surroundings, a series of passive and dynamic meditation facilitates one to:

◆ Replenish frozen tears with Warmth and Love.
◆ Hurts with Healing Touch.
◆ Rigidity with Flowingness & Childlike Innocence.
◆ Receiving with Giving.
◆ Seriousness with Playfulness.
◆ Knowledge with Wonderment.
◆ Confinement with Celebration.
◆ Withholding, with Let Go... in order to nurture one's 'being' centred in Restfulness.

For more details on Swamiji's in-house & public workshops, contact:

PRASANNA TRUST
51, Ground Floor, 16th Cross,
Between 6th & 8th Main
Malleswaram, Bangalore 560 055, India
Tel: +91 80 4153 5832-35, Fax: +91 80 2344 4112
E-mail – prasannatrust@vsnl.com
prmadhav@vsnl.com
Visit us at www.swamisukhabodhananda.org
www.prasannatrust.org • www.ohmindrelaxplease.org

NIRGUNA MANDIR
#1, Nirguna Mandir Layout, Near I Block Park,
Koramangala, Bangalore – 560 047, INDIA
Phone: (080) 2552 6102

Name: ....

Title ....

Company ....

Address ....

....

City ....

State .... Pin ....

Telephone ....

Fax ....

Email ....

Please send me information on
☐ Seminar on LIFE program
☐ Workshop on E-Lab Program
☐ Seminar on Oh, Mind Relax Please!
☐ Seminar on Corporate Harmony & Creativity at work
☐ Books Audio Cassettes, CD's, VCD's

I know a few people who want to be benefited from Swamiji's program. Their names & Contact numbers are:

Name: ....

Tel: ....

Mobile: ....

City: ....

E-mail: ....

Name: ....

Tel: ....

Mobile: ....

City: ....

E-mail: ....

Name: ....

Tel: ....

Mobile: ....

City: ....

E-mail:...